39

D0899035

Meeting Procedures

*Parliamentary Law and Rules
of Order for the 21st Century*

James Lochrie

THE SCARECROW PRESS, INC.
Lanham, Maryland, and Oxford
2003

SCARECROW PRESS, INC.

Published in the United States of America
by Scarecrow Press, Inc.
A Member of the Rowman & Littlefield Publishing Group
4501 Forbes Boulevard, Suite 200, Lanham, Maryland 20706
www.scarecrowpress.com

PO Box 317
Oxford
OX2 9RU, UK

British Library Cataloguing in Publication Information Available

Library of Congress Cataloging-in-Publication Data

Lochrie, James, 1944–
    Meeting procedures: parliamentary law and rules of order for the 21st
century / James Lochrie.
        p. cm.
    Includes bibliographical references and index.
    ISBN 0-8108-4423-0 (cloth : alk. cloth)
    1. Parliamentary practice. I. Title.
JF515 .L68 2003
060.4'2—dc21

2002012024

Printed in the United States of America

∞™ The paper used in this publication meets the minimum requirements of
American National Standard for Information Sciences—Permanence of Paper for
Printed Library Materials, ANSI/NISO Z39.48-1992.
Manufactured in the United States of America.

Dedicated to my wife Christina, who cajoled, encouraged, and begged me to finish this book. Now she has no fear of presiding at a meeting.

Also to the Richard Kain parliamentary forum on Yahoo.com, whose members often kept me wondering how many motions one could legitimately cram into one item of business.

Contents

~

Foreword

Rules can be abstruse, and none more than the rules of meetings. They frighten people, scare them, and for the average presiding officer they can turn a pleasant afternoon into a nightmare—but this need not be so. This book is designed to keep rules simple. Explanations are clear, and many examples are included. The author's generous use of tables help to clarify matters further. It is certainly not a *Robert's Rules of Order*, but it does cover the material required for the typical meeting participant and presiding officer. Even the busiest presiding officer and the individuals who attend meetings probably ever see only a small fraction of the rules used. This reasonably short book is all that is required to ensure that a meeting will accomplish its purpose.

I learned a lot, knowing Jim Lochrie for approximately eight years and serving under his leadership as president of the American Institute of Parliamentarians. In the two years he led the organization I watched him preside with calm demeanour. He respected the rights of his board, permitted all members to discuss issues, and when the situation called for a dash of humor, he delivered.

Jim understands perfectly the fundamental rights of all members in a meeting. He is not a stickler for the rules. He enforced the rules when necessary, but more often than not he was flexible in his presiding duties, thus allowing everyone to relax and enjoy the meeting. What is most important, he got the business accomplished.

I urge you, the reader, to take this book with you to meetings and use it. It will help you not only understand what is happening but participate in the decision-making process. No longer will lack of knowledge require you to be silent.

Thanks to Jim for providing this useful book.

Teresa A. Dean, PRP, CPP-T
President, 2001–2003
American Institute of Parliamentarians

~

Preface

Groucho Marx is reputed to have said that he would never join an organization that would have him as a member. This may be so, but it is not the sentiment of tens of millions of volunteers who join and participate in millions of not-for-profit organizations across North America and in democracies worldwide. These organizations vary in size from the very small, less than ten members, to a few hundred, to a few thousand, to the hundreds of thousands; some have memberships of a million or more. There are book clubs, soccer clubs, gardening clubs, religious groups, and groups of such professionals as nurses, doctors, massage therapists, scientists, astronomers, actors, and many, many more. The need to organize, to join, to participate in a group is a human characteristic—and in North American society, a passion. We organize into groups because we have interests. We can support and promote these interests by working with persons with like interests.

Some organizations have as members other organizations. The local bowling club may be a member of a county or city bowling association, which in turn may be a member of the state or provincial association, which in turn may be a member of the national association. Each level from local up to national and international usually has its own constitution or bylaws, policies, procedures, meetings, and executive or management.

There are a myriad of ways in which these hierarchical organizations may relate to each other, but there is one constant in all of the challenges and politics that occur within not-for-profit organizations—that decisions must be made that advance the aims of the organization. It is a feature of not-for-profit organizations that most of these decisions are made at meetings. That is the essence of this book. It is about meetings, but not meetings in isolation. It is about advancing the aims of the organization through good decision making, supported by due process and procedure.

The rules of procedure implement the principles of democracy. Democracy is about fairness, equality of opportunity and treatment, justice, and self-rule. "Self-rule" simply means that the members of the organization set the rules by which fairness, equality, and justice are attained. The rules are set by using such concepts as open access to information, due process, freedom of speech, majority rule, courtesy, order, efficiency, and minority rights. These concepts and many more are explained and expanded in this book. Of course, the concepts and rights mentioned are not as simple as that. We could simply say to a president of an organization, "You make the decision." This would be super-efficient but would rub violently against due process, majority rule, and freedom of speech, to mention a few democratic precepts. There needs to be a balance; that is the challenge of democracy, and the challenge of defining organizational procedure.

This is not a guidebook. It is a prescriptive book. It defines rules that may be adopted by a democratic organization. It is a modern text on meeting procedure, taking into consideration new communication technologies and, more importantly, the modern business practices of organizations. It avoids jargon by building on the advances of late-twentieth-century English-language usage in parliamentary law.

Although the book is prescriptive in nature, it relies heavily on principles. It is important to understand the principle behind a rule, because rules can be abused and misinterpreted. When this occurs, and it occurs often, the principle can be invoked. In some cases no rule may exist to cover a specific situation. Again the principles of meeting procedures may be invoked.

The book is organized as follows. The first chapter defines the fundamental principles of parliamentary law and introduces the most important concepts of meetings, explaining them in some detail. The second chapter defines the various documents of authority that are required by an organization to ensure efficient, effective, and legal operation. These include bylaws, rules of order, and policy. The third chapter introduces the order of business and agendas. Chapters 4 through 9 cover all motions, including main motions, subsidiary motions, privileged motions, and incidental motions. It lays out the various rules associated with these motions in tables that are easily accessible and understandable. Chapters 10 and 11 are on voting, nominations, and elections. It introduces the concept of the vote-counting protocol, showing the various ways by which votes are turned into results or social decisions— the essence of democracy. Chapter 12 covers annual meetings and conventions and, in particular, the various committees required. Chapter 13 provides answers to questions that have been posed to the author by associations.

I thank Christina Scott Marshall Kay for editing many of the chapters. Thanks also to John Stackpole, a professional parliamentarian whom I consulted with on chapters 10 and 11—"Voting Methods," and "Nominations and Elections." He changed my thinking in some key areas. Where I did not take advice, I expect to be corrected in the future. In all cases the final decision was mine and mine alone.

I also thank the many associations that I have worked with over the years, who have taken my advice and reinforced my belief in the democratic process. It has been a wonderful sixteen years serving them.

James Lochrie
October 2002

~

CHAPTER ONE

Principles and Rules at Meetings

The following sections lay out the many concepts and principles that apply to meetings. It explains the general principles of parliamentary law, the legal meeting, notice of meeting, quorum, the presiding officer, the secretary, attendees, observers, debate, speaking, formality and informality, discipline in meetings, and conflict of interest. These are not all the rules that apply to meetings but those that are fundamental to orderly and effective meetings. Rules regarding specific motions are covered in later chapters.

General Principles of Parliamentary Law

The fundamental essence of a meeting is the equal opportunity of members to initiate ideas, oppose ideas, and to do so without coercion. Six principles underlie the rules of any meeting. These are:

1. The majority must be allowed to rule.
2. The minority have rights that must be respected.
3. Members have a right to information to help make decisions.
4. Courtesy and respect for others are required.
5. All members have equal rights, privileges, and obligations.
6. Members have a right to an efficient meeting.

Not all the principles listed above are absolute. For example, in certain circumstances, such as closing debate, there may be a requirement to adopt a motion by a two-thirds vote. This abrogates the rights of the majority to rule (the first principle) and the members' right to information (third principle). However, it reinforces the members' right to an efficient meeting (sixth principle). The right of the majority to rule and the membership's right to information are balanced against the right to an efficient meeting.

Other important rights—such as the right to discuss issues freely, to deal with one item of business at a time, and to advance notice of business—are derivable from these six principles. Detailed rules of procedure and other parliamentary concepts are also derivable from these principles.

The Majority and the Minority

Thomas Jefferson said, in his first inaugural address as president, on March 4, 1801, "All, too will bear in mind this sacred principal, that though the will of the majority is in all cases to prevail, that will, to be rightful, must be reasonable; that the minority possess their equal rights, which equal law must protect, and to violate which would be oppression." Here Jefferson addresses the fear of many of the tyranny of the majority. The majority rules through the ballot box, by its voting power, but its actions must be reasonable. When its actions are unreasonable, the majority may be seen to have abused its right to rule; the consequences are civil unrest and, in the extreme, even revolution. The minority needs to be safeguarded not only through the principle of protection of the minority but through that of equal opportunity to avail itself of the law.

Parliamentary law has many written rules of which the minority may avail itself. These rules—such as the right to debate, the right to information, the right to vote, the right to attend, the right to receive advance notice, the right of the absentee to protection, and many more—all serve to protect the minority. Again, these rights are not absolute. The right to information may not be taken to such an extreme that the minority ties up decisions. Thus debate may be cut off to ensure the right to an efficient meeting. In this way the majority is protected from the minority.

The key to balancing the rights of the majority and the rights of the minority is *reasonableness*. The rules that protect the majority, allowing it to rule, and the rules that protect the minority, allowing it to oppose, provide reasonableness in practice. One of the important concepts in parliamentary law is that the constituents of an organization set their own rules for reasonableness. In one organization five minutes of debate per person may be reasonable, while in another three minutes, or twenty minutes, may be reasonable. The decision depends on the nature of the organization. Receiving an agenda two days before a meeting may be reasonable and adequate in one organization, while in another organization a month is needed.

The Right to Information
A meeting generally trades nothing except information. It is the currency by which decisions are made; appropriate and reliable information must be available if the decisions are to be effective. Each member in a meeting must have factual information. This information comes from debate, committee reports, advisors, and the experience of members. When sufficient information is not available to make informed decisions, there are mechanisms in parliamentary law by which to seek it. These mechanisms include postponing a decision to a later time, referring a decision to a special committee (either to act or recommend back to the meeting), and consulting with specialists (who are given advisor status). In addition, informal debate and vigorous formal debate will help crystallize useful information and opinion.

The right to information is not limited simply to receiving the information; the information must also be timely. Agendas, reports, and important decisions to be considered must generally be known prior to a meeting. Time must be allowed for analysis. Surprising members with last-minute decisions to be made is inappropriate and may be considered an unreasonable restriction on the members' right to information.

Courtesy and Respect
The one right of every member—and, it could be argued, nonmembers too—that may never be restricted is the right to hold an opinion. An opinion may be swayed through information and logical argument, but never ridiculed by word or action. Each member's opinions must be re-

spected and afforded the courtesy of a hearing. Ridicule, harsh words, or personal attacks may cause a member to lose face, which in turn may lead to failure to contribute information or participate to the fullest in the organization. The rules of decorum in debate are important in maintaining the rights of members with regard to courtesy and respect. Interruptions of speakers are generally prohibited and must be dealt with immediately, as matters of the highest priority. Even when interruptions are allowed, members who are discourteous or disrespectful of other members should be brought to order. All members must be on alert for infractions of decorum. There are remedies in parliamentary law against members who behave in a disrespectful manner against other members. These include being brought to order by the presiding officer, being made to apologize, and if necessary, being expelled from the meeting.

Equal Rights, Privileges and Obligations

Members have equal rights and privileges with respect to meetings. They have rights to advance notice, to attend meetings, to speak in debate, to make motions, to vote, to make nominations for office, and to run for office. These rights are not absolute but can be restricted in certain ways in the interest of reasonableness. The important point is that restrictions on rights apply to all members. For example, the right to run for the office of president may be restricted with respect to experience, but the requirement must apply to all members.

Certain obligations come with membership in any organization. Some of these are embodied in the rules of particular organizations and may vary. However, other obligations are common to all organizations. The most important of these are the obligations to abide by the rules of the organization and to abide by decisions reached in legal meetings. Members are obliged not to oppose decisions already made except through proper parliamentary mechanisms, such as moving to rescind or reconsider them. If the member cannot in good faith abide by a decision, that member must decide between living with it or leaving the organization.

Right to Efficient Meetings

Members are entitled to an organized and efficient meeting. There are many rules in parliamentary law that protect the efficiency of meetings and allow members to insist upon it. Members have a right to an agenda and to see that agenda followed; members must strictly adhere to the subject of debate and may be called to order if they do not; members must address only one thing at a time; if a subject is complex, members may have it discussed in a smaller and more efficient forum (a committee); time limits may be placed on debate; debate may be closed; and motions may be set in an order of precedence. All of these rules make for efficient meetings.

The presiding officer and the members are all guardians of the efficiency of the meeting. A presiding officer who is well versed in parliamentary law and the skills required by the office can move through the agenda efficiently and make the meeting a pleasant experience. An efficient meeting, however, is not an absolute right but must be balanced by the effectiveness of the meeting —that is, its ability to reach useful and well thought out decisions. The presiding officer must take care to permit meaningful debate. Debate may be extended to enhance effectiveness, even at the expense of efficiency. This is a balancing act that the presiding officer and the members in attendance must play at each meeting.

Legal Meetings

A meeting of an organization will generally be considered "legal" if all members entitled to attend were notified sufficiently in advance of its time and place, a quorum of members is in attendance, the meeting has been called to order at the notified time or later, and a presiding officer and secretary are present or are appointed at the meeting.

The concepts of "time and place," "in attendance," and "present" have been recently modified by statute because of rapid changes in communication technology. Unless the bylaws of an organization otherwise provide, a meeting may be held by means of telephone or other electronic communication systems that permit all persons participating in the meeting to communicate with each other simultaneously and instantaneously. A meeting may no longer be limited to a physical location but may be distributed over locations many miles apart, provided that all persons participating can hear each other at the same time and can respond to all participants at the same time. Anyone participating in such a meeting is deemed to be present at it.

Types of Meetings

Three types of meetings are significant in parliamentary law:

- The regular meeting

- The special meeting

- The continued meeting

The calling of regular and special meetings is normally defined in the organization's documents of authority, usually the bylaws. The continued meeting is defined as a meeting that continues business from a regular or special meeting from the point at which the earlier meeting adjourned. A continued meeting is set through a motion to "fix the time to continue the meeting" (see chapter 8). It is not necessary to provide notice for a continued meeting, unless the documents of authority require it. It is legally an extension of the original meeting at a different time and, if necessary, a different place.

The major characteristic of a special meeting is that the business to be conducted is defined in the call to the meeting. No other business may be conducted, even by unanimous consent of those present.

Notice of Meeting

Members have a right to know that a meeting has been called and at what place and time. The specific procedure for providing notice of meetings should be contained in the organization's documents of authority. The method of calling annual or general meetings should be in the bylaws. The procedure for calling board meetings may be contained in board rules, and for committees in committee rules. Scheduling regular meetings by resolution a number of months ahead constitutes notice, provided all members have been notified. In all cases, however, including special or emergency meetings, the rules for calling meetings must be well defined in some document of authority.

Time lines are likely to be shortened in special or emergency circumstances, but an attempt must be made to contact and notify all members. For emergency meetings a different quorum may be defined in the documents of authority to make such meetings legal. In this instance, the definition of an emergency meeting must be well established.

Quorum

A quorum is a defined representation of members required to conduct business legally. Its purpose is to avoid making decisions with an un-representative group of members. Quorum representation should be es-tablished in the bylaws. If the bylaws are silent, a quorum is a majority of members in good standing. (See the definition of a member "not in good standing" below, under "Discipline at Meetings.")

A quorum may be defined as an absolute number or as a percentage of the membership. There are pros and cons of defining the quorum ei-ther way; each organization needs to think carefully how best to define its quorum. In small groups, such as committees or boards, a quorum defined as a majority of the members in good standing is usually appro-priate. This would be inappropriate, however, for a national organiza-tion with thousands of members, of whom only a few hundred could be expected to attend annual meetings.

A quorum may also be defined in terms of both numbers and specific member categories. For example, a quorum for an organization may de-fine a quorum as a hundred members representing at least forty coun-ties. For emergency meetings of an executive committee the quorum may be defined as seven members, three of whom must be officers. These types of quorums are called *qualified quorums*, because they are qualified as to specific member types.

A member who has declared a conflict of interest and leaves the meeting is not counted in determining the quorum. If the member re-mains in the meeting, even though not voting, the member is counted in determining the quorum.

A quorum must always be present if legal business is to be con-ducted. It is the duty of the presiding officer and the obligation of each member to bring to the attention of the meeting the loss of a quorum. If this occurs, the meeting may recess to restore the quorum, set a time for a continued meeting, or adjourn.

A meeting may be called to order in the absence of a quorum, but no business may be conducted. However, procedural items may be dealt with, reports may be heard (but not acted on), information may be given, and program or social aspects of the meeting may be carried out. In such a case, though business has not been conducted, a meeting has taken place, and its minutes are to be written, distributed, and filed in accordance with normal practices of the organization.

Presiding Officer and Secretary

The presiding officer, who is usually the president of the organization, has duties prior to, during, and after a meeting. During the meeting the presiding officer must protect all rights of those attending, allowing the majority to rule and the minority to be heard, and ensure that decorum in remark and action is maintained, that the agenda is followed, and that the meeting progresses with due efficiency. Members have the same obligations, but the presiding officer is looked to in the first instance for leadership during the meeting.

The presiding officer must treat all members and others in attendance with respect and courtesy, recognizing them to speak when appropriate, maintaining a manifest neutrality when assigning the floor, answering questions, offering information, and ruling on points of order. Patience is truly a virtue. The presiding officer must be evenhanded in word and action, showing no negativity toward any participant.

A presiding officer who is required, or wishes, to make a motion or speak in debate must vacate the position and participate as a regular member of the meeting. The position of presiding officer is then filled by the president-elect or the vice president, or in accordance with the documents of authority. If the president-elect or the vice president has already spoken on the subject at hand, they must decline to preside. When the item of business is complete, the regular presiding officer again takes up the gavel. The only circumstance in which the presiding officer as such may debate is in response to an appeal from a decision of the chair. In committees or small boards the presiding officer is normally allowed to participate in debate and make motions without vacating the position.

If the presiding officer is not present, the president-elect, if there is one, presides. If there is no president-elect or the president-elect is also absent, the vice president presides. In the event none of these officers are present, the meeting elects, by majority vote, some other person to preside.

Some organizations use a professional presiding officer who is a non-member. This arrangement should be stated in the documents of authority; if the documents of authority are silent, the members may appoint, by majority vote, a nonmember to preside. A nonmember who presides does not vote.

Presiding is a learned skill, and there are many rules and techniques upon which the presiding officer can rely. A few of these rules and techniques are:

1. Always state the motion after it has been seconded (this is a rule).
2. Always state the motion just before taking the vote (a rule).
3. State the motion at frequent intervals, especially if discussion is lengthy or the parliamentary situation is complex.
4. Have the vice president or staff (discussed below) keep track of the order of speakers.
5. Take notes and use the secretary to help keep track of the pending motions.
6. Alternate between speakers for and against, where possible.
7. Insist that members address all remarks through the chair (a rule).
8. Ask members to state whether they are for or against the motion, so as to focus the members on what is being said.
9. Use the five words, "If there is no objection . . ." to deal with trivial changes to motions or inconsequential procedural matters.
10. Stay out of the business at hand. Vacate the chair in favor of the president-elect or vice president if there is a need to participate personally in the discussion (a rule, discussed above).
11. If unsure how to proceed, ask the members.
12. Use the gavel to open and close the meeting.
13. Be pleasant, patient, and helpful.
14. If discussion becomes repetitive, ask, "Are you ready for the vote?"

15. If members are unruly (chattering), ask the member who is speaking to stop until they stop. It is thus usually unnecessary to ask the chatterers to stop; they will normally quiet down on their own. If they do not, call them to order (a rule).
16. Avoid debate before a motion is on the floor (a rule).
17. On a point of order, if you are unsure how to rule you may turn the question over to the meeting for decision (a rule).
18. If you make a mistake, stop the proceedings, state your error, correct it, then move on.
19. Do not turn over the meeting to someone (say, a committee or staff member) who is reporting; maintain control at all times. Continue to state motions that arise, call for discussion, take the vote, and announce the result.
20. To maintain the necessary degree of neutrality, vote only if your vote will make a difference.

Unless the documents of authority state otherwise, the presiding officer has a vote and may exercise it; there are two circumstances under which the presiding officer's vote will make a difference. If the vote is tied, the presiding officer may either vote in favor of the motion or, if opposed, announce that the motion is lost or defeated. In addition, the presiding officer may vote to make a tie, thereby defeating the motion. A nonmember presiding officer has no vote and may not take any such action.

Secretary

The principal duty of the secretary at a meeting is to record all acts of the assembly and subsequently produce minutes of the meeting for approval at the next meeting. If a meeting refers business to a committee, the secretary provides the committee all documentation required to carry out its duties. The secretary also has the duty to ensure that all officers or other members who are assigned actions during the meeting are given appropriate instructions. The secretary, who sits next to the presiding officer, can be invaluable to the presiding officer by keeping notes on pending business and, when required, sharing that information with the presiding officer and the meeting participants. The secretary may debate, make motions, and vote on all matters.

The secretary has many other duties outside of the meeting, including keeping most records of the organization (except financial records), recording incoming and outgoing correspondence, maintaining the documents of authority and the minute book, ensuring that all records required by regulatory or government bodies are filed, submitting necessary records to the parent body if there is one, and filing appropriate records of constituent units.

Minutes

The minutes of an organization, when approved by the meeting, are the official and legal record of the acts of the assembled membership. A court may subpoena the minutes, and unless evidence to the contrary is presented, it will consider them a factual statement of what occurred at the meeting.

Minutes should be concise and clearly written so that anyone not present at the meeting would understand what occurred. They are also an excellent source of history for the organization.

They are a record of what was done, not what was said. Unless it is traditional in the organization and except for courtesy resolutions, the minutes need not indicate who made a motion or who seconded it.

The minutes, in order to provide an accurate and fair representation of the meeting, must contain the following information:

1. The name of the organization or committee.
2. The type of meeting (regular, special, continued).
3. The date and time of the meeting.
4. The location where the meeting was held.
5. The name of the presiding officer and secretary.
6. The time the meeting commenced.
7. The roll call (names), if a roll call was conducted.
8. A statement that a quorum was present.
9. The disposition of previous minutes and corrections made.
10. Reports of officers.
11. Reports of standing committees.
12. Reports of special committees.

13. For all substantive main motions the exact text as voted on and the disposition, whether adopted, defeated, postponed to a later time, or referred to a committee.
14. Points of order and the presiding officer's rulings.
15. Appeals from rulings of the presiding officer and whether sustained or reversed.
16. All counted votes, listing the number for and the number against the motion.
17. On a roll-call vote, the names of all members answering the roll call and how they responded (Yes, No, Abstain).
18. In elections, all persons accepting nomination for a position.
19. In elections, the complete teller's report.
20. In elections, the result of the election as announced by the presiding officer.
21. All advance notices.
22. The names of all appointees to committees.
23. All actions assigned, whether to a committee or an individual.
24. The time the meeting adjourned.
25. The secretary's signature.

The minutes do not normally contain the following information:

- The points made in debate

- Who made the motion, unless it is customary to record the maker of the motion

- Who seconded the motion

- Procedural motions, such as to limit debate, close debate, or suspend the rules

The presiding officer has discretion as to what may be recorded by the secretary. For example, if a member is named for disciplinary reasons, the presiding officer should instruct the secretary to note the offending remarks or actions. The members may also, by general consent or a majority vote, record in the minutes specific remarks made in debate. Appendix A contains sample minutes.

Attendees at Meetings

An attendee at a meeting is ordinarily a person who is present. For electronic meetings, a person who can communicate and respond to all other attendees simultaneously is an attendee. The right of a member to attend a meeting is inherent in membership in the organization, group, or committee. For that reason all members have a right to notice of the meeting.

Persons who are not members have no right to attend, except as may be contained in the documents of authority. However, many persons who attend meetings are not members. Their right to attend has normally been established by precedent. However, if there is a dispute as to who may attend, the assembly may by majority vote permit a nonmember to attend. Likewise, a nonmember may be granted permission to speak, by general consent or by majority vote.

The attendees at a meeting, for purpose of discussion, may be categorized as follows:

- Members or delegates[1]

- Staff

- Consultants

- Observers (and guests)

A *member* of an organization is defined in the organization's document of authority. Members or delegates have all the rights of membership at a meeting as granted by the documents of authority. At a minimum, they have the rights to attend, speak, make motions, vote, and run for office.

In a *delegate meeting,* which is a subset of the larger membership, members who are not delegates often have the right to attend and, by permission of the assembly, to discuss motions or ask questions. It is unusual to extend other rights, such as to make motions or nominations

---

1 In a meeting of delegates, nondelegate members may be present, but only with restricted rights.

to office, to members who are not delegates. The documents of authority should lay out the rules for nondelegate members in this respect. If the documents of authority are silent, a nondelegate member has no rights at a meeting—even to attend.

Staff personnel are an important part of most meetings. They are instrumental in ensuring a smoothly run meeting, by supporting the officers and other participants with information and handling the logistical and physical aspects of the meeting. However, unless the documents of authority provide otherwise, staff take no substantive part in the meeting. Their rights are equivalent to those of invited consultants.

The major function of a *consultant* is to provide information and advice to the officers and to the meeting generally. The most common consultants at a meeting are lawyers, parliamentarians, and specialists in the subject under discussion. A consultant does not debate or advocate but may state a position based upon knowledge and experience. Consultants have no right to take part in the meeting, even though invited; they may address the meeting only when asked to do so. A consultant may seek permission to speak; permission is usually given through general consent or, if necessary, a majority vote.

Observers are persons who have received general invitations to attend; guests, in contrast, have received specific invitations. Guests are often dignitaries from the community or affiliate organizations and are often introduced at the beginning of the meeting. Observers and guests have no rights beyond that of attendance, which may be withdrawn by majority vote.

In general, unless the documents of authority state otherwise, any nonmember may be excluded from all or part of a meeting by majority vote. If a right of a nonmember to attend a meeting is contained in the bylaws, a two-thirds vote is required to exclude. The issue often arises when members have been given, through the documents of authority, the right to attend board meetings. Another example is when nondelegate members have been given the right to attend a delegates' conference. Although members of the organization, they are not members of the specific body; when this occurs a two-thirds vote to exclude is required. This action is equivalent to suspending a rule of order in the documents of authority.

Debate

Debate is regulated discussion. Advocacy of a position on an issue is debate; unsolicited provision of information to a meeting is debate. A nonmember providing information on a subject does not constitute debate. Asking a question is not debate. Depending on the formality of the meeting, debate is regulated under strict rules of order. For formal meetings the rules are:

1. Debate may not begin until the presiding officer has stated the motion.
2. Permission to speak, and hence to debate, is required from the presiding officer.
3. Debate must be germane to the issue or subject under debate.
4. Debate must be courteous and respectful, and no one may impugn the motives of another.
5. Persons debating must adhere to time limits set by the meeting rules. If the rules are silent a person may not speak for more than five minutes to each motion.
6. Persons debating must adhere to the number of times the meeting rules says a person may speak to each motion. If the rules are silent a person may not speak more than twice to each motion.
7. If the rules permit a person to speak more than once to a motion, that person may not speak a second time if a person who has not yet spoken to the motion is seeking the floor.
8. A person debating a motion may not in closing remarks make a motion to limit or close debate, or to adjourn the meeting.
9. The presiding officer may not (as discussed above) debate a motion without first turning over the presiding position to another who has not debated. When the subject has been disposed of, the presiding officer may resume the gavel.
10. Members with conflicts of interest may not debate the subject.
11. The presiding officer or (with the permission of the presiding officer) a member may make brief remarks on nondebatable motions.
12. The presiding officer or a member may interrupt a speaker on a point of order if the member believes the speaker is violating a rule of debate.

A member who believes the formal rules of debate, as stated above, are interfering with the efficiency or effectiveness of the meeting may propose, a suspension of a specific rule or rules (not rules 4, 10, or 12) of debate. This suspension requires a two-thirds vote. Rule 4, 10, and 12 may not be changed even by unanimous vote. A member in a conflict-of-interest position (rule 10) may, if asked, provide factual information but may not debate or advocate a position.

In some meetings, including committee and small boards, debate may be informal. The attendees set their own degree of formality, depending on the nature of the meeting and the significance of the decisions being made. The following rules of debate apply in small assemblies:

1. Discussion may take place in the absence of a motion.
2. Permission to speak is not required, and a member may speak as many times as required.
3. There are no time limits on speeches.
4. The motion to close debate is not permitted.
5. The presiding officer is permitted to debate and make motions.
6. Debate must be germane to the issue or subject under debate.
7. Debate must be courteous and respectful and may not impugn the motives of members.
8. Members having conflicts of interest may not debate the subject.
9. The presiding officer or a member may interrupt a speaker on a point of order if the member believes the speaker is violating a rule of debate.

The above rules of debate for informal meetings will normally work in meetings of fifteen or less members, sometimes more. If it appears during the meeting that informality is impeding progress or interfering with effectiveness, the presiding officer or a member may propose a change in the rules of debate. By general consent or majority vote the rules, except for rules 7, 8, and 9, may be changed.

Permission to Speak

In most cases, a person attending a formal meeting must be recognized by the presiding officer before speaking. When recognized, the member is said to have exclusive ownership to speak. Exclusive ownership to speak may be gained by right but is more often assigned by the presiding officer.

There are two situations in which a member has exclusive ownership to speak over another member. These are:

- A member who has made a motion has the right to speak first to the motion.

- A member who has not yet spoken on a subject has the right to speak before a member who has already spoken to it.

In each of these cases, the member who holds the right to speak must claim the right before someone else is assigned that right and begins speaking. The presiding officer, even after recognizing someone else to speak, may give the floor to a member who owns the right to speak, provided the other person has not actually begun speaking. It is always incumbent upon the individual member to claim the right to speak, as the presiding officer normally cannot know which members wish to speak.

When two members rise to speak together, the first to address the presiding officer is entitled to recognition. In some meetings, because of the size of the assembly, the physical attributes of the meeting place, or the use of electronic devices, recognition to speak may require more elaborate procedures, which should be defined in a document of authority.

A nonmember who wishes to address the assembly must seek permission in the same manner as a member with the right to speak. This permission to speak is granted through general consent or by majority vote of those voting.

There are a number of instances when a member may speak without permission. These are:

1. When seconding a motion, a member may call out "Second."
2. A member who is unsure of a vote result, either prior to the announcement of the vote or after it is announced by the presiding officer, may call out, "I doubt the vote."

3. A member who believes the group has departed from the agenda may call out, "Follow the agenda," or "Point of order."
4. A member who wishes to make a point of order, point of privilege, or appeal a ruling and interrupting the speaker is warranted, does so by addressing the presiding officer.

Formality in Meetings

Formality in a meeting pertains to the degree to which a group adheres to the normal rules of procedure. In large groups, to maintain order and efficiency, many rules are adopted and strictly followed. In small groups a minimum of rules are adopted, and some flexibility is usually allowed. Order is usually less important in a small group than in a large group. In a large group disorder will quickly lead to confusion; it will be difficult to bring the meeting back to order. The rules of large groups are usually intended to ensure an orderly process of business. Groups larger than thirty require a high degree of formality and strictness in procedure. Groups smaller than fifteen can often operate with a minimum of formality. Groups between fifteen and thirty persons should lean to more formality to provide flexibility in operation.

Finding the right degree of formality for a group is sometimes difficult. It is better, however, to err on the side of more formality than on less; relaxing formality is easier than increasing it. A group has the power to change its own rules of procedure. Adopting a slightly stricter set of rules than actually required allows the presiding officer and the group some leeway in finding the level of formality suitable to the group.

Throughout this book, rules of procedure are defined for formal meetings and for informal ones, but groups need to find their own levels of formality to optimize order and efficiency. The fundamental principles of meetings—such as courtesy and respect, majority rule, minority protection, the right to information, and equality of rights and privileges—must be adhered to whatever the degree of formality of the group.

Discipline at Meetings

Members at a meeting must abide by the rules of the meeting as contained in the organization's documents of authority. Failure to do so may result in disciplinary action. The usual reasons for discipline at a meeting are:

- Being disruptive through continual interruptions

- Making offensive remarks and being disrespectful to others

- Using unparliamentary language and harsh words or tone

- Impugning the motives of others

- Not following the legitimate orders of the presiding officer

The presiding officer, as the leader of the group, should take prompt action to ensure that the rules are being followed. If the presiding officer fails to take such action, any member may do so through a point of order, bringing to the attention of the presiding officer the alleged behavior. The presiding officer is required to rule on the point of order or refer the matter to the assembly.

The presiding officer should point out minor infractions of the rules to people breaking them. If the infraction is minor, such as using an intemperate word, the presiding officer may wait until the person has stopped speaking, but the presiding officer always has the right to interrupt a speaker.

The purpose of discipline in a meeting is not to punish offending members but to change their behavior. The presiding officer should be cautious and measured in imposing discipline. Cautious escalation provides an opportunity for the member to refrain from harmful conduct before it gets serious enough to warrant the most serious of sanctions, expulsion from the meeting.

The escalation of remedies is as follows:

1. The presiding officer requests that the member refrain from breaking the rules, specifying the infraction or the rule being broken. Nothing more need be done if the member complies.

2. If this fails, the presiding officer provides a sterner warning by calling the member to order. This is a clear instruction from the presiding officer that the member must refrain from continuing any adverse action and, if necessary, to be seated. Nothing more need be done if the member complies.

3. If after this clear instruction the member continues with the disruptive action or refuses to be seated the presiding officer may, if the breach of conduct is serious enough, call upon the assembly to take action. The presiding officer says, "What sanctions do the members wish to take against [names the member]?"

If the situation has reached the third level of escalation and the presiding officer has named the member, any other member may make a motion asking that the offending member apologize, be censured, be expelled from the meeting, or be assigned any other combination of sanctions appropriate to the breach of conduct. (At this stage in the proceedings, suspension or expulsion from membership is not permissible.) The secretary, if requested, reads from the minutes the actions of the member as evidence of the breach of conduct. The member is permitted briefly to make a defense of his conduct. A majority vote adopts the motion.

If an apology is ordered, it is to be given at that time. If the member refuses, the presiding officer may order the member to leave the meeting until an apology is forthcoming. If censure is ordered, the organization should issue it according to its normal rules. A censure is a verbal or written rebuke, or both. It is intended to show the assembly's disapproval of and displeasure with the acts or remarks of a member. If expulsion from the meeting is ordered, the presiding officer may establish and appoint a committee to escort the member from the meeting room. The escorting committee may not touch the offending member; if the member refuses to leave, the appropriate civil authorities should be called.

Even more emphatic action, which may extend to suspension or expulsion from membership, may be taken against a member who has caused a serious breach of conduct in a meeting. This further action must be carried out under the regular disciplinary procedures of the organization.

A member suspended from membership is no longer in good standing. The documents of authority should specify what rights are removed from members not in good standing and how the members may be restored to good standing. If the documents of authority are silent, the rights removed are those to attend business meetings (which by implication removes the rights to speak, make motions, and vote) and to run for office.

Conflict of Interest

In a meeting, a *conflict of interest* exists when a member must choose between a potential personal gain and the interest of the organization. The personal gain is defined as a benefit to the member, the member's family, or to business associates.

The interest of the member may be real or potential. In either case, the member must declare the conflict as soon as possible. The purpose of disclosing even potential conflict is to improve the likelihood that it will not hurt the organization.

It is not wrong in itself to have a conflict of interest. In our capitalistic society, in which commerce is all-pervasive, conflicts of interest must be expected to arise from time to time. For an item of business (a contract, transaction, decision), what is important is that conflicts be declared and that members declaring conflicts remove themselves from any dealings with the subject in question. It is unreasonable to expect such individual to resign from the organization.

If a conflict is disclosed properly and the member refrains from debating and voting on the subject, and leaves the meeting, the organization may, by vote, still award business to the individual or declare the conflict inconsequential.

A member cannot be accused of having a conflict of interest but only of failing to disclose it. Taking part in debate and voting on a matter in which the member has an undisclosed interest may lead to disciplinary action. These charges would follow the regular disciplinary procedure adopted by the organization. Sanctions for nondisclosure of a conflict of interest may vary from censure through fines to termination of membership. Sanctions imposed must be reasonable in the specific circumstances, and in all circumstances the membership must follow prescribed procedures that protect the rights of the member being investigated.

CHAPTER TWO

~

Documents of Authority

Definitions and Terms

- Documents of Authority—Instruments of law or of an organization that empower or restrict an organization in its activities and that are intended to be permanent until expressly changed. They represent the written will or agreement of the body that enacts the document. Documents of authority are not all equal but have an order of precedence of authority (as explained below).
- Statute—A law enacted by the legislative branch of a government. This includes delegated legislation, such as rules and regulations enacted by various branches of the government or quasi-government authorities.
- Charter or Articles of Incorporation—A written instrument from a state granting certain rights and privileges to operate an enterprise. It includes, among other things, the name of the enterprise and the objectives that the enterprise intends to pursue. Depending on the enterprise, it may also set forth restrictions on operation.
- Constitution or Bylaws—An adopted set of rules that regulate the structure of an organization, its internal affairs, the governance of its members, and its relationships with external entities.

- Rules of Order—The detailed rules of parliamentary procedure that govern the operation of the organization's meetings. They pertain to the orderly conduct of business, the right of members to information, the efficiency and fairness of business, the rights of the majority, and the rights of the minority.
- Special Rules of Order—Rules of order adopted by an organization that replace certain rules of order contained in the organization's parliamentary authority.
- Parliamentary Authority—A written text containing an extensive set of rules of order that the organization has adopted.
- Fundamental Rules of Order—A subset of rules of order that is considered so fundamental to democratic principles that specific rules within the subset may not be suspended under any circumstances.
- Policy—The detailed rules of an organization dealing with the administration and operation of the organization. These rules or policy do not normally contain rules of order for meetings.
- Delegated Rules—Rules or policy that are delegated by a higher authority to be formulated and enforced by a lower authority. For example, the bylaws may delegate a committee to develop and maintain a set of policy.
- Suspension of Rules—A procedure used in a meeting to suspend temporarily a rule of order that is interfering with the conduct of business. When the reason for suspending a rule is no longer applicable, the suspended rule is again applicable.

Documents of Authority

Documents of authority are not only ranked in order of precedence but may have different rules for amendment, such as the notice period and the vote required to amend. Certain rules within a document of authority may also be suspended, while others may not. The table below shows the order of precedence, the rules for amendment, and the rules for suspension for the different documents of authority. The order of precedence (ranking) is shown from the highest (1) to the lowest (6). An organization has little or no control over statutes; however, they are included in table 2.1 for the sake of completeness.

Table 2.1. Attributes of Documents of Authorities

Precedence or Rank	Document or Instrument	Notice Required to Amend	Vote Required to Amend	Vote Required to Suspend
1	Statute	Not applicable	Not applicable	Not suspendable
2	Charter or articles of incorporation	Yes[1]	2/3 vote[1]	Not suspendable
3	Constitution or bylaws	Yes	Majority[2]	Not suspendable unless a section or rule contains a provision for its own suspension[3]
4	Special rules of order	No	2/3 vote	2/3 vote[4]
5	Parliamentary authority	Not applicable	Not amendable[5]	2/3 vote[4]
6	Custom or unwritten rules	No	Majority	Majority

1. This is the notice or vote required by the members of an organization to recommend an amendment to the charter. The actual approval of the amendment is through a government agency.
2. Some organizations may have separate constitution and bylaw documents. The constitution often requires a two-thirds vote to amend.
3. Constitution and bylaws often contain rules of order. These rules of order in the constitution and bylaws may be suspended by a two-thirds vote even though they do not contain a provision for their own suspension.
4. There is a certain class of rules that are not suspendable. These are the fundamental rules of order that are not suspendable under any circumstances. These are described in this chapter.
5. Although the parliamentary authority is not directly amendable, a rule of order in the parliamentary authority may be replaced by a special rule of order.

Statutes and Charters

A provision or rule in a statute takes precedence over a provision or rule in the corporate charter. A provision or rule in a charter takes precedence over all other documents of authority in an organization. One of the most important provisions in a charter is that stating the objectives of the corporation. They are often broadly phrased, to allow the greatest freedom of operation. One aspect of the objectives of an organization relevant to parliamentary law is that a member may not introduce through a motion or notice business that lies outside the scope of the objectives of the corporation, except with the approval of a two-thirds vote of the organization. This approval may be given by the members in assembly or by the board.

Some statutes control an organization even to the extent of regulating rules of order. For example, quorum requirements, proxy voting, the vote required for the corporation to act, and conflict-of-interest provisions are often contained in statutes or government regulations. It is incumbent on the organization to be aware of those rules, which take precedence over any adopted parliamentary authority or special rule of order.

Constitution or Bylaws

The constitution and bylaws constitute the primary document, or documents, over which an organization has control. Within this parliamentary authority the words "constitution" and "bylaw" are interchangeable; many organizations have a single document entitled "Constitution and Bylaws." Organizations that have two documents often distinguish the documents by the vote required to amend them, with the constitution requiring a two-thirds vote and the bylaws a majority vote. To avoid inconsistencies between the two documents it is recommended that an organization adopt a single document, the bylaws.

The essential nature of bylaws is that they define the internal structure of the organization and in particular the authority conferred upon the board, its officers, and its standing committees. The members retain authority not conferred through the bylaws. The bylaws are a contract between each member in the organization and as such may be changed only at a members' meeting, under a strict amendment procedure.

An organization must determine for itself the content of its bylaws. The content is normally set out in well-defined articles. The articles themselves may be subdivided into sections. Bylaws should specify only "what" is to be done, not "how." For example, the bylaws may specify what elections are to be held, who is to be elected, and under what conditions. The details of the election process should be delegated to the board or a committee, through a rule in the bylaws—for example, "The board shall adopt and publish a nomination and elections process for officer and board of director positions, and may amend it from time to time." This format for delegation of authority may be used throughout the bylaws.

The following are suggested articles for bylaws:

Article 1, Name
This article establishes the exact name by which the members wish the organization to be known. If the organization is incorporated, the name must be the legal name of the corporation as listed in the corporate charter. However, this article may be omitted if the organization is incorporated.

Article 2, Objectives
The second article lays down the objectives of the organization and its scope of operation. The objectives should be concise and should avoid specifying how the objectives are to be met. If the organization is incorporated, the article must include the objectives of the corporation as listed in the corporate charter. Again, this article may be omitted if the organization is incorporated.

Article 3, Definitions
This article lists and defines the meaning of terms that are unique to the organization, have a different meaning from common usage, or are to be interpreted in particular ways. For example, this section may define such terms as "client," "year-end," "retired member," "nonvoting member," "region," and "not in good standing." Such terms may be defined within other sections of the bylaws, but if used in many places throughout the bylaws, it is useful to collect their definitions in a single place.

Article 4, Members
This article defines the organization's membership categories, the criteria for membership in each category, the dues for membership, who

sets the dues, and the membership year. The procedure for joining the organization and for the payment of dues should be defined in a subordinate document of authority.

Article 5, Board of Directors and Executive Committee

This article defines the structure and authority of the board of directors and, if an executive committee is required, the structure and authority of the executive committee. The "board of directors" and "executive committee" are sometimes known by other names. Essentially the board, subject to the bylaws, controls the organization between members' meetings, whereas the executive committee, again subject to the bylaws, controls the organization between meetings of the board.

The article further defines the number of members of the board, how they are elected or appointed, and their terms of office. It may also define any rotational method of filling the positions from year to year. The article should also specify circumstances under which a board member may be removed from office and how a vacancy, however caused, is to be filled.

Article 6, Officers

The sixth article defines the officer positions (as a minimum usually the president, the vice president, secretary, and treasurer), how they are elected or appointed, and their terms of office. The article should also specify how an officer may be removed from office and how a vacancy, however caused, is to be filled.

Article 7, Meetings

This article defines the following different types of meetings:

- Members' meetings

- Board of director meetings

- Executive committee meetings, if required

- Committee meetings

One of the members' meetings should be defined as the *annual meeting*. The annual meeting hears reports from the officers, the board, the auditor, and standing committees. At the annual meeting elections are held for officer positions, board positions, and where required, other important positions within and external to the organization. The annual meeting is often a delegate meeting, one in which delegates of the organization's membership at large are authorized to act on behalf of the organization at large. Delegate meetings are covered in chapter 12.

For each of these types of meetings this article defines:

- Who may call the meeting
- The notice required
- The quorum requirement
- The regularity of the meetings
- Special meeting requirements
- Who may attend meetings

More than one method by which a meeting may be called should be provided for. It is not useful simply to state that the "president may call the meeting." Other methods, such as "petition by six members of the board" or "by two members of the committee," should also be given. This allows flexibility in the event of an emergency or crisis.

Notice must be reasonable; what is reasonable depends on the type of meeting and the nature of the organization. The notice periods may be different for a regularly called meeting and an emergency or special meeting. Once a notice period is defined in the bylaws, it may not be suspended.

The concept of quorum is discussed in chapter 1. Great attention must be given to setting the quorum requirement, as once established it may not be suspended.

In defining the regularity of the meetings it is wise to provide some flexibility as to meeting dates. A bylaw clause that says, for instance, "The executive committee shall meet on the first Tuesday of each month" should provide an escape clause such as, "unless varied by a majority vote of the executive for a specific month."

Special meetings most often apply to members' meetings but, depending on the nature of the organization, may also be defined for board, executive, and committee meetings. Special meetings must be defined in terms of who may call the meeting, the notice period required, the quorum requirement (usually the same as for a regular meeting), and the agenda. The agenda is of particular importance for the special meeting, as we have seen, in that no item of business may be brought up at the meeting that is not specified in the agenda, not even by unanimous consent of those present.

Some organizations distinguish between a "special" meeting and an "emergency" meeting. In this case the meaning of an emergency meeting must be well defined and understood. Like a special meeting, an emergency meeting must be formally called, but the notice period may be shortened, and the quorum may be reduced and qualified.

All members of a body have the inherent right to attend the meetings of the body. In some cases it may be prudent to extend the right to attend to nonmembers. A statement of the right of a nonmember to attend should specify how that right may be removed. For example, a rule might stipulate that "a nonmember's right to attend a committee meeting may be removed by a majority vote of the committee."

This article may also authorize the use of mail balloting or electronic mail balloting and specify the vote required for the body to act. This approach essentially allows some bodies to formally act without a meeting, with certain restrictions.

Telephone or electronic meetings (see "Legal Meetings," chapter 1) may also be authorized, provided that these types of meetings are allowed in the jurisdiction under which the organization operates.

Article 8, Committees

This article lists the standing committees that have been assigned specific areas of responsibility and that continue from year to year. As a minimum the bylaws should specify the business area assigned to each committee and whether it has power to act in particular instances. If the bylaws are silent on the power to act, the committee has no authority other than to meet, formulate policy, and report its recommendations to the board or the members for final decision.

The method of appointment of the chair and members of the committee may be specified in bylaws but may instead be defined in a subordinate document of authority, such as board rules.

This article should also provide an enabling clause that allows the board to establish special committees to carry out specific assignments. A special committee may also be given the power to act. A typical clause might read, "The board of directors may establish a special committee to investigate, report and recommend to the board action to be taken. A special committee may be given the power to act." If the bylaws are silent on the establishment of special committees, the board has no authority to establish such committees.

This article should also list and define such bodies as past-president councils, advisory boards, and other such bodies, as required.

Article 9, Elections

This article defines how nominations and elections for officer positions, board positions, and if required, important committee positions are to take place. For example, if a process of nominations other than from the floor is required, it should be specified in the bylaws; although nominations from the floor are normally always permitted, they may be disallowed by a clause in the bylaws—a practice that is not recommended. Likewise, elections by default use a majority of the votes cast to elect; if another method of counting the vote is required, it should be specified in the bylaws. The detailed nomination or election procedure need not be in the bylaws but may be placed in a subordinate document of authority.

Article 10, Discipline

An organization, by the nature of its business, may need to discipline its members and thereby may be required to impose sanctions or penalties on members from time to time. This article should authorize the procedure by which the organization may discipline its members. It should also specify the range of sanctions or penalties it may impose—fines, censure, suspension, or expulsion from membership. The detailed procedure for disciplining a member should be specified in a subsidiary document of authority.

Article 11, Parliamentary Authority
This article specifies the adopted parliamentary authority of the organization. It contains the rules of order that the organization will follow when other documents of authority—for example, bylaws and special rules of order—are silent. The article need not be specific as to the edition of the book. The article would read, "The current edition of [book title] is the parliamentary authority of [organization] and shall govern it except where inconsistent with governing legislation, the corporate charter, the bylaws, or any special rules of order adopted by [organization]."

Article 12, Dissolution
The article on dissolution provides for an orderly dissolution of the organization. It should specify the distribution of assets of the organization. In most voluntary organizations, particularly charitable or not-for-profit ones, assets do not accrue to the members on dissolution; the power of distributing the assets is normally given to the board. The board would follow the instructions provided in this bylaw article. It is advisable to have a lawyer draft this article.

Article 13, Amendments to the Bylaws
This article specifies the rules under which the bylaws may be amended, as follows:

• Notice requirements

• The vote required to amend

If the bylaws are silent on notice requirements for amending the bylaws and this book is adopted as the parliamentary authority, notice must be given at the last previous meeting or in the written call to the meeting. The call to the meeting should follow the normal procedure for the organization or be reasonable as to the timeliness of notice to the members. If the bylaws are silent on the vote required to amend the bylaws, it is a majority of the votes cast, a quorum being present.

For example, this article may read, "The bylaws may be amended by a majority vote provided two weeks written notice of the specific bylaw amendment is given to the members by mail to the address on record at headquarters."

It defeats one of the fundamental premises of bylaws to make them subject to continual amendment. It may be wise to restrict amendments to once per year at the annual meeting and permit other amendments only at special meetings called for the purpose of amending the bylaws. This makes it difficult to amend the bylaws, but does leave the option open, if the members wish to call a special meeting for that purpose.

Special Rules of Order

The rules in the parliamentary authority cover many of the situations that occur in meetings. An organization may, however, need to vary the rules of the parliamentary authority or fill gaps in the rules where the parliamentary authority is silent. In these cases the organization may adopt special rules of order. The special rules take precedence over the parliamentary authority. These special rules may not be inconsistent with the bylaws, the corporate charter, or legislation. Special rules require a two-thirds vote to adopt or amend and a two-thirds vote to suspend for a specific purpose.

Normally, special rules of order are adopted for specific bodies of an organization. For example, a board of directors may adopt special rules for the conduct of their board meetings, or a convention may adopt special rules for the conduct of the convention. In either case, it is the rules of the parliamentary authority that are being varied. Board special rules and convention special rules need not bear any resemblance to each other; they are adopted to meet the specific needs of that particular body.

Some authorities use the term *standing rules* to connote special rules that continue from meeting to meeting. This book calls "special rules" those rules that are expected to continue from meeting to meeting, especially when the body meets frequently. Convention special rules are normally adopted each time the convention convenes, because the body of delegates change from convention to convention and the convention is only convened once per year, perhaps even less often.

Boards often adopt rules that do not pertain to rules of order but refer to a board policy that applies to meetings. For example, there may be a dress code that applies to board members, or a rule that disallows the wearing of perfume or scent at a meeting. These examples are in essence board policy (see "Policy," below). This type of policy requires only a majority vote to adopt or amend and a majority vote to suspend for a specific purpose. A convention set of rules may also contain policies that only require a majority to adopt or amend and a majority vote to suspend for a specific purpose.

If, as is often the case, the rules are a mixture of special rules of order and policy, a two-thirds vote is required to adopt them. Subsequently rules of order may be added or replaced by a two-thirds vote, and policy by a majority vote.

Parliamentary Authority

The parliamentary authority has the lowest order of precedence (ranking) of the written rules. The parliamentary authority to be consulted is normally specified in the organization's bylaws. If the bylaws are silent a parliamentary authority may be adopted, by a majority vote without notice, at the beginning of a meeting, after the establishment of a quorum. If a parliamentary authority is not adopted, either through the bylaws or by motion, common parliamentary law applies. This is the set of parliamentary rules that have been established through court cases or custom. However, average participants of a meeting cannot be expected to know the common rules, so establishing a parliamentary authority is imperative. Most organizations eventually run into situations in meetings that are not readily overcome except with the assistance of a comprehensive parliamentary authority.

Custom—Unwritten Rules of Order

An organization may have certain rules of order that are unwritten but customary. For example, when elections are pending and nominations have been completed, the members typically expect the candidates to give short speeches. If by custom it is the right of each candidate to speak, the right may not be denied a candidate because it is unwritten. An organization may have many such rules; each such rule has the same authority as a written one.

However, if an unwritten rule or rule of custom clashes with a written rule in the bylaws, the special rules of order, or the parliamentary authority, the unwritten rule is of no weight and falls to the ground. If when a rule of custom is being followed a member points out a conflicting written rule in the parliamentary authority, that rule must be followed. The assembly may adopt an unwritten rule as a special rule of order thereby making it higher in precedence than the parliamentary authority.

Fundamental Rules of Order

A rule of order once adopted may be suspended by a two-thirds vote. Suspension is normally required when a rule interferes with the efficiency or effectiveness of the meeting. For example, the parliamentary situation may be so complex that the participants at a meeting become confused and do not know how to proceed. In this case the rules may be suspended to discard the current pending motions and start afresh. (*The Standard Code of Parliamentary Procedure*, by Alice Sturgis, calls this tactic "cutting the Gordian knot.")

There is, however, a set of rules that may not be suspended in any circumstance. These are:

1. Bylaws, unless they allow for their own suspension.
2. Rules that protect a minority—even a minority of one.
3. Vote-counting protocols (chapter 10).
4. The requirement for a ballot vote.
5. The quorum requirement for a meeting.
6. Notice requirement for a meeting.
7. Notice requirement for a motion or proposal.
8. Special meeting agendas, which may not be amended as to content, though they may be amended as to order of taking up items of business.
9. Rules of decorum, including any rule that relates to respect and courtesy toward individuals or groups.

Policy

The policies of an organization may range from the organization's loftiest beliefs and philosophy to the mundane administrative rules of the organization. To be effective, policies must be written and understood by those who use them. They are the business rules that drive the organization. Policies are often substantive rules that affect the success of the organization in crucial ways and that must be followed. They are often categorized in such areas as finance, membership, public relations, administration, staff, ethics, environment, and privacy, to name a few.

Policies are adopted by the members in assembly or by the board of directors, or they may be delegated to specific committees or to staff members. The nature of the organization dictates how policy is adopted. If adopted at a meeting, it normally requires a majority vote and may be amended or rescinded by the same vote. In some cases, elements of policy may be mentioned in bylaws, but the bylaws should be concerned only with delegating the authority for categories of policy to the most appropriate bodies within the organization—board of directors, committees, or staff.

Policy is not concerned with rules of orders for meetings, although it may apply to meetings. For example, there may be a policy regarding payment of expenses for attending board meetings or how a member must dress when attending a meeting (a dress code).

As noted in an earlier part of this chapter, a board may adopt as board rules a mixture of rules of order and policies. Rules of order that vary from the parliamentary authority require a two-thirds vote to adopt, while policy normally requires a majority. If the board is to adopt the rules en bloc, a two-thirds vote is required. Subsequently to add or amend a rule or policy requires either a two-thirds or a majority vote, depending on the nature of the rule.

CHAPTER THREE

~

Order of Business and Agenda

Definitions and Terms

- Order of Business—The framework and sequence of categories of business that an organization will ordinarily follow in setting an agenda. The order of business should be defined in a document of authority.
- Agenda—The specific items of business to be dealt with at a meeting. The items are placed on the agenda in the sequence defined by the order of business. The agenda would ordinarily be unique for each meeting.
- Business Item—Those agenda items that if adopted in a properly constituted meeting establish the policy, procedure, rules, and decisions of the organization and constitute an act of the organization.
- Program Item—Those agenda items that do not constitute an act of an organization but pertain to educational, social, or other matters that an organization may arrange from time to time.
- Convention Program—All the planned events of a convention. This includes business meetings, educational and social events, and any other event that the organization may wish to arrange. It is usually planned and scheduled meticulously, particularly where overlapping or parallel activities are involved.

Order of Business

The purpose of an order of business is to establish a stable sequence of business, one that permits an agenda to be constructed readily and in a sequence that is not confusing to participating members. To enhance the stature of the order of business, it should be defined in a document of authority.

The general sequence of an order of business is to deal first with business items brought forward by officers and committees, followed by business yet to be completed from previous meetings, then new business, followed by program items.

Each organization should establish an order of business that meets the needs of the organization. If it is not contained in the documents of authority and the organization has adopted this book as its parliamentary authority, the following is the order of business:

1. Call to order
2. Opening ceremonies
3. Approval of minutes
4. Report of officers
5. Report of boards, standing committees and special committees
6. Business carried forward from previous meetings
7. New business
8. Announcements and good of the order
9. Adjournment

The order of business for a body of the organization should be placed in a document of authority over which that body has control. For example, the board has control over its own board rules; therefore, the order of business for board meetings should be placed in board rules. This allows the board to change its order of business by majority vote.

The person or persons charged with constructing the specific agenda for a meeting would use the adopted order of business as the framework into which particular items of business would be placed. Although all business may be placed in the order of business as stipulated above, there may be logistical or expedient reasons for varying from the established order. The members in assembly may vary the order of business and any particular agenda item by a majority vote. This may be done through the adoption of the agenda at the beginning of the meeting or, if necessary, during the meeting.

Call to Order

With one rap of the gavel, the presiding officer, after gaining the attention of the assembly, announces, "The meeting will come to order." This establishes that the meeting has begun but does not establish that business may be conducted. The presiding officer establishes that a quorum is present immediately after calling the meeting to order. This may be done through a roll call of members or by simply announcing, "A quorum is present," if it is clear that in fact a quorum is present. A quorum is assumed to be present throughout the meeting unless the contrary is brought to the attention of the assembly and subsequently verified. The presiding officer and all members have a duty to call to the attention of the assembly the lack of a quorum at any time. If it is established that a quorum has been lost, no further business can be conducted, except at the risk of members present. If action taken by members at an inquorate meeting (a meeting without a quorum) is not ratified at a meeting with a quorum, the members present at the inquorate meeting are personally responsible for the action, not the organization.

If at the beginning of or during the meeting it is established that a quorum is not present, the assembly may take a recess, set a date for a continued meeting (chapter 8, "Fix the Time to Continue the Meeting"), or adjourn. It may continue the meeting, but it may not conduct business other than to hear reports, announcements, or conduct the program, if any.

Opening Ceremonies

After the call to order the presiding officer conducts opening ceremonies, which may consist of an invocation, an acknowledgement to the state, an introduction of special guests, an opening statement by the presiding officer, any ritual that the organization has approved, or all of the foregoing.

Approval of Minutes

The secretary may read the minutes; if they have previously been circulated to the members, the reading may be dispensed with. The presiding officer asks, "Are there any corrections to the minutes?" If there are no corrections the presiding officer continues, "There being no corrections, the minutes are adopted as read [or circulated]."

In the event that corrections to the minutes are offered, the presiding officer may make an initial determination by saying, "The correction is noted, and the secretary will make the correction." At this point any member may disagree with the correction being made, by so stating. If the matter is not resolved informally, the presiding officer shall assume a motion to correct the minutes (or have the member make a motion to correct). If the presiding officer is unsure whether the correction should be made when first brought up by the member and remains uncertain after informal discussion, the presiding officer shall ask the member wishing the correction to make a formal motion to correct the minutes. The motion to correct the minutes requires a second, is debatable, is amendable, and requires a majority vote to adopt. Once a motion to correct the minutes has been made and voted on, the presiding officer will take a vote on the minutes as a whole.

If for any reason a series of minutes comes before the meeting, the oldest are dealt with first, proceeding in turn to the most recent.

After the minutes have been approved, the secretary signs and dates the minutes (date of approval).

Chapter 1 and Appendix A provide additional information on minutes.

Report of Officers
The report of an officer is for information only and deals only with the administrative duties and activities of the officer. If an officer requires a decision of the assembly, the matter may properly be placed under new business or in another appropriate place on the agenda. When the report is complete, the presiding officer asks, "Are there any questions or comments on the report?" The questions, comments, and answers may not go into discussion or debate but, again, are for information only. If the officer's report is written, it is filed. If the report is oral, a short description is noted in the minutes. If the treasurer reports on the status of the finances of the organization, the report is filed for audit. No substantive motions may be made during the report of officers.

Report of Boards, Standing Committees, and Special Committees
The report of a board or committee may contain recommendations, motions, or resolutions that it presents to the assembly for adoption. Appendix B shows a report format a board or committee may use. The recommendations would normally be dealt with when the board or committee reports, but they may be placed under new business or at another appropriate place on the agenda. The chair of the board or committee, or a designate, makes the report and after reporting makes the motion or resolution the committee wishes to present for adoption to the assembly. The committee motion does not require a second, but all other procedural matters dealing with the handling of motions are followed.

The full textual report of a committee need not be adopted unless the committee's report is to be published. "Published" here means that the report is to be accessible to the general public or to an external organization, or that it has been designated as an official record of the organization by the organization.

If a committee member or members wish to present a minority report to the assembly, they may only do so by general consent or by majority vote of the assembly. The minority report is for information only and may be presented only after the report of the committee. To act on the minority report requires a motion to consider it in place of the committee report. Whichever report is to be considered, any subsequent motion made may be amended or have any subsidiary motion applied to it.

Business Carried Forward from Previous Meetings
This deals with unfinished business from any previous meeting and includes:

- Actions taken away from a previous meeting by an individual

- Business postponed to a future meeting

- Business not completed or reached at a previous meeting

Actions taken away from a meeting must be reported at a subsequent meeting. The intention at the meeting is not to resolve the action but to report its disposition. If the action has not been completed, a new date for its completion is set, and the action is carried to the next meeting. No debate or substantive motion is permitted at this point in the agenda, other than informal discussion regarding the disposition of the item and any new date for disposition. The item may, however, be disposed of at the current meeting by being placed under new business.

Business postponed to a meeting is listed on the agenda in the date order it was postponed, the oldest items listed first.

Business interrupted by adjournment or not reached is listed on the agenda in the order in which it would have been dealt with at the previous meeting.

New Business

The rules for introducing new business to an assembly should be defined in the organization's documents of authority. If the documents of authority are silent on the matter, the following rules apply:

- Any item of business may be introduced by motion or resolution, with or without notice, when the presiding officer calls for new business.

- Any motion introduced under new business that amends or rescinds something previously adopted requires the same vote and notice that adopted the motion.

- Any motion introduced under new business that does not amend or rescind something previously adopted requires a majority vote to adopt, unless the documents of authority state otherwise.

- If a motion is introduced under new business that requires notice to adopt and notice has not been given, the presiding officer will rule the motion out of order.

- Items brought up under new business that has previously been referred to a committee shall be ruled out of order. However, a member may move to take the motion from the committee (see chapter 4, "Remove a Decision from a Committee").

Announcements and Good of the Order

This part of the order of business allows members and officers to make announcements pertaining to relevant events or happenings that may be of interest to the members. It may also be used for congratulatory speeches, commendations, or for suggesting ways of improving the organization. No motions, other than courtesy resolutions, are permitted during this part of the agenda. It is intended to be an informal but useful part of the agenda.

Adjournment

This part of the order of business may be reached before all items on the agenda are dealt with. A member who wishes to adjourn moves the motion to adjourn when no business is pending (see chapter 8, "Privileged Motions"); the presiding officer has a duty to remind the members of the business still to be conducted. Having done that, the presiding officer takes the vote on the motion to adjourn. If adopted, the presiding officer may make relevant announcements prior to declaring the meeting adjourned. If the motion fails, the business continues where it was interrupted.

Once all items on the agenda have been dealt with, the presiding officer may ask for a motion to adjourn or may assume a motion to adjourn. If the motion is adopted, the presiding officer declares the meeting adjourned.

Agenda

Members have a right to information. The agenda is the organization's official vehicle for providing members with the detailed information of business that will come before a meeting. When the agenda is sent to the member prior to the meeting, the member is better informed and may better prepare for the meeting. The agenda follows the framework provided by the order of business.

The responsibility for preparing the agenda lies with the presiding officer of the meeting, unless varied by the documents of authority. The presiding officer may use other officers, chairs, or staff to compile the agenda but maintains responsibility notwithstanding. The presiding officer must place on the agenda all business items required by the documents of authority, requests from officers, requests from committee chairs who are ready to report, all items carried forward from a previous meeting, all items of business postponed from previous meetings, and requests from any member of the body who wishes to introduce an item of new business.

Although it is neither normal nor necessary to time an agenda, it may be necessary to conduct certain items of business at a specific time or within certain time frames. For example, at annual meetings, it is important that nominations and elections of officers be completed; it is therefore advisable to set a time in the meeting for the nominations and elections to be conducted. The presiding officer has discretion as to placing agenda items in certain time frames or at specific times on the agenda. When the time arrives for a timed agenda item, the presiding officer interrupts the current business and takes it up. When the timed agenda item has been completed, the meeting takes up the item of business that was interrupted. To vary the time of a timed agenda item requires a two-thirds vote.

Although the order of business dictates the placement of an agenda item, the presiding officer is afforded some discretion when dealing with scheduling or logistical problems of the meeting. This is particularly relevant when some special business or emergency business must be dealt with. When the order of business is varied because of such matters, the presiding officer seeks approval of the agenda through general consent or, if necessary, a motion and vote at the beginning of the meeting. A vote, if required, requires a second, is debatable, and requires a majority to adopt. If the agenda requires amendment during the meeting, the presiding officer seeks to amend by general consent and, if necessary, by majority vote.

The agenda should be as detailed as necessary to permit a member to prepare. Reports of officers, committees, and the wording of motions, if known, are included in the agenda. In addition, it is good practice to note for each item on the agenda the action required by the assembly. The most common annotations are "adopt/reject" and "for information only."

Consent Agenda

A *consent agenda* is a list of noncontroversial items of business that may be acted upon by the meeting by a single motion. The consent agenda may be developed by the presiding officer or the executive committee; it is taken up and acted upon in the regular agenda after the approval of minutes. It is an efficient method of dealing with a list of uncontentious items.

The presiding officer, upon reaching the consent agenda, takes each item of business on the consent agenda and asks, "Does any member wish to hold this item for discussion?" A member wishing to hold an item would state, "Hold." This is a demand and must be complied with. If held, the consent agenda item is placed on the regular agenda at the place in which it would normally be taken up. Having covered all items on the consent agenda, the presiding officer assumes a motion by stating, "The motion is on the adoption of those items on the consent agenda. All in favor say 'aye' [pause]; those against say 'no.' The ayes have it, and the consent agenda is adopted."

~

CHAPTER FOUR

Main Motions

Definition and Terms

- Motion—A formal proposal by a member that the assembly take particular action. It is usually introduced by a member with the words, "I move that . . ."
- Substantive motion—A motion whose content is related to the business of the organization. For example, a main motion or a resolution that proposes the adoption of a policy by the organization would be substantive.
- Procedural motion—A motion whose content largely affects procedural aspects of a meeting. For example, motions to take a recess or to make a point of order are procedural motions.
- Main motion—A substantive proposal made by a member. It is the lowest ranked motion and may only be made when no other business is pending.
- Resolution—A main motion more formally presented.
- Subsidiary motion—Motions that modify the main motion or in some way assist in disposing of the main motion. The subsidiary motions in order of rank, lowest to highest, are to postpone indefinitely, amend, refer to a committee, postpone to a certain time, limit or extend debate, close debate, and postpone temporarily.

- Privileged motions—Motions that must be dealt with immediately even if business is pending. The privileged motions in order of rank, lowest to highest, are to raise a question of privilege affecting an individual, raise a question of privilege affecting the assembly, recess, adjourn, and fix the time to continue the meeting.
- Incidental motions—Motions that are mainly procedural and relate to the rules of order, information, the efficiency of the meeting, or voting methods. There is no rank order of incidental motions (see chapter 9).
- Assumed motion—A motion assumed by the presiding officer when it is obvious what the next action of the meeting is to be. For example, if a committee reports its intention to present a number of motions, the presiding officer may assume those motions in the order indicated.
- Pending business—All motions that have been stated or allowed by the presiding officer but have not yet been disposed of.
- Currently pending business—The last motion stated or allowed by the presiding officer that has not yet been disposed of.
- Order of precedence of motions—A ranking of motions. If a motion is pending, only a motion of higher rank (or precedence) may be proposed.
- Germaneness—In debate, a speaker must speak to the pending motion. A speaker's remarks may be ruled out of order if they are not germane to the topic. Germaneness also applies to amendments. An amendment must in some way be associated with or relevant to the motion being amended. If it is not, the amendment may be ruled out of order and disallowed by the presiding officer.

Order of Precedence

The order of precedence of motions is given, from lowest (the thirteenth) to highest (the first) in table 4.1.

Incidental motions (see chapter 9) do not have an order of precedence and are not shown in the table. Incidental motions apply in many different situations and take precedence over the motion to which they apply at the time they are made.

Table 4.1. Order of Precedence of Motions

Type of Motion	Motion	Ranking
Main Motion	Main Motion (s)	13
Subsidiary	Postpone Indefinitely	12
Motions	Amend	11
	Refer to a Committee	10
	Postpone to a Certain Time	9
	Limit or Extend Debate	8
	Close Debate	7
	Postpone Temporarily	6
Privileged	Raise a Question of privilege-individual	5
Motions	Raise a Question of privilege-assembly	4
	Recess	3
	Adjourn	2
	Fix the Time for a Continued Meeting	1

If a motion to refer to a committee (rank ten) is pending, motions of types one through nine may be proposed. Motions eleven through thirteen would be ruled out of order. A motion to amend the main motion would be ruled out of order, but because "amend" also applies to the motion to refer, a motion to amend the number of members on a committee, for example, would be in order.

A common format will be used to discuss each motion in this chapter and in chapters 5 through 9. Tables will be used throughout to define the characteristics and precedence, respectively, of the individual motions. Table 4.2 lists seven characteristics.

Chapters 4 through 9 use precedence tables to explain, for each motion:

- The motions over which the motion takes precedence

- The motions to which the motion yields

Using the main motion as an example, the format of the precedence table is as shown in table 4.3.

The precedence table is logical for the thirteen ranked motions, because the ranked motions have, by definition, an order of precedence. However, the precedence table is usually complex for incidental motions,

Table 4.2. General Table Format for Motion Characteristics

Characteristic	Required	Further Explanation
Second	Yes or No	Specifies whether a second is required for the motion.
Debatable	Yes or No	Specifies whether debate is allowed for the motion. This row also specifies whether debate is restricted and in what manner it is restricted.
Amendable	Yes or No	Specifies whether a motion may be amended or changed. Motions that have a variable in them are generally amendable.
Vote Required	Majority or Two-thirds or Other vote	Specifies whether a vote is required, whether the vote required is a majority, a supermajority or some other percentage. Requests do not require a vote, unless they are moved as a motion.
May Interrupt	Yes or No	Specifies whether a speaker may interrupt another speaker to make a motion. Most motions do not permit the speaker to be interrupted.
May Be Renewed	Yes or No	Some motions when defeated may be made again but only when the parliamentary situation has changed. Motions that have been adopted cannot be renewed but some may be reconsidered.
May Be Reconsidered	Yes or No	Specifies whether a vote may be reconsidered. This parliamentary authority only permits substantive main motions to be reconsidered. This row also provides information on how the result of a motion may be reversed.

Table 4.3. Precedence Table (Main Motion)

Takes Precedence Over:	Yields To:
No other motion. May be made only when no other motion is pending.	All other motions, except another main motion.

because incidental motions do not have an inherent order of precedence. In addition, incidental motions may be applied to any of the thirteen ranked motions or to other incidental motions. In practice, to determine which motions yield to which other motions, it is best to think in terms of the last pending ranked motion (one to thirteen).

For example, assume the following motions are pending:

- A main motion

- An amendment to the main motion

- A motion to recess

- A request to withdraw the main motion

The two ranked motions that would be now in order are a motion to adjourn and a motion to fix the time to continue the meeting, because they are of higher rank than the motion to recess. In this example, the motion to withdraw would yield to motions to adjourn or fix the time to continue the meeting. In standard wording, and according to the precedence table, the situation is: "The incidental motion yields to the motion to postpone temporarily and all privileged motions, provided these motions are of a higher precedence than the last ranked motion pending. It also yields to other incidental motions, provided they are truly incidental to the meeting situation at that time."

Using the example above, a request for information (an incidental motion) would be in order if it regarded the meaning of the motion to withdraw. However, an incidental motion to consider the main motion paragraph by paragraph would be out of order, because it is not truly incidental to the current situation.

Main Motion

A *main motion* formally brings a substantive proposal before the meeting for decision by the members. A main motion stated by the presiding officer introduces a subject for the first time or may reintroduce the subject from a previous meeting (see table 4.4).

Table 4.4. Main Motion

Characteristic	Required	Further Explanation
Second	Yes	A main motion proposed by a committee need not be seconded.
Debatable	Yes	Is fully debatable and may go into all aspects of the question.
Amendable	Yes	Amendments must be germane to the original motion but may be hostile to the original intent.
Vote Required	Majority	A main motion normally requires a majority vote to adopt. Some organizations may, through their documents of authority, require a supermajority to adopt depending on the nature or content of the motion. For example, bylaws often require a two-thirds vote to adopt an amendment to the bylaws.
May Interrupt	No	A main motion has the lowest order of precedence and may be made only when no motion is pending.
May Be Renewed	No	A main motion, that has substantially the same intent or content, is not renewable within the same meeting after it has been adopted or rejected. It may, however, be reconsidered.
May Be Reconsidered	Yes	Both a negative and an affirmative vote may be reconsidered. See motion to Reconsider (chapter 4) for addition information.

Procedure and Example

After being recognized by the presiding officer to speak, the member says:

1. "I move that we donate five hundred dollars to the local children's fund."
2. Another member, without being recognized, seconds the motion. If the motion is not seconded, the presiding officer says, "Is there a second?" If the motion is not seconded the presiding officer says, "There is no second, the motion is not before you."
3. If a member seconds the motion the presiding officer says, "It is moved and seconded that we donate five hundred dollars to the local children's fund. Is there any discussion?"
4. Discussion may go into the merits of the motion, but it must be germane to the intent of the proposal.

5. After discussion, the presiding officer repeats the main motion before taking the vote, saying, "The motion is that we donate five hundred dollars to the local children's fund. All those in favor say 'aye' [pause]; all those against say 'no' [pause]. The ayes [or noes] have it, and the motion is adopted [or defeated]."
6. The presiding officer continues with the next business, in order.

A common format for a main motion is a *resolution*. A resolution is made up of a preamble (one or more "whereas" clauses) followed by one or more "resolve" clauses. The preamble only provides background to the resolution and generally avoids any points that may be debated. The resolve portion of the resolution, like any main motion, describes the action its proponents are asking the organization to take. By way of example, the format of a resolution is:

Whereas, Our organization is twenty years old next July;
Whereas, Our parent organization has decreed that all constituent units take all opportunities to promote our cause; and
Whereas, We have been invited to take part in the bicentenary celebrations for our city next July,
Resolved, That we participate in the parade that is planned by the city;
Resolved, That a committee of seven be set up to organize our participation; and
Resolved, That a budget of five thousand dollars be set aside for the event.

A main motion in the form of a resolution is dealt with in the same manner as any other main motion, except that the resolve part of the resolution is open to amendment before the preamble part is, because the resolve clause is the more important part of the resolution. Amending the resolve clauses first avoids any inconsistency between the preamble and the resolution.

A *courtesy motion* is normally presented in the form of a resolution, except that no negative vote is taken by the presiding officer.

The precedence of main motions is summarized in table 4.5.

Table 4.5. Precedence Table (Main Motion)

Takes Precedence Over:	Yields To:
No other motion. May be made only when no other motion is pending.	All other motions, except another main motion.

Other Considerations

If it is known that a main motion is to come before the assembly, it is good practice to include the wording of the motion in the notice of meeting. If the exact wording is not known, the subject of the proposal should be given.

During the consideration of the motion, the presiding officer should repeat the motion often enough to keep the members informed and focused on the proposal. As a minimum, the motion should, as noted above, be repeated just prior to the taking of the vote.

A main motion should be written out in full and presented to the presiding officer. Some organizations adopt rules to this effect. Motion forms should be completed in duplicate and contain, in addition to space for the text of the motion, blanks for the names of the maker of the motion and seconder. Both the presiding officer and secretary receive copies.

The main motion can be kept displayed in front of the members at all times by an overhead projector or computer-generated graphic.

Main Motion—Amend a Previous Decision

A motion to *amend a previous decision* brings a substantive proposal that has been previously decided back before the meeting for a new decision by the members. Such a motion, when adopted, amends a policy, procedure, or rule of the organization. It becomes effective immediately upon adoption unless qualified by a proviso or another motion. If the motion fails, the previous decision remains in effect. Such a motion may be used to amend a decision that has been partially executed, but it does not nullify or affect in any way any action that has already been carried out under that decision.

An assembly that undertakes to amend a previous decision of the organization must have authority to do so. If an assembly amends a previous decision without having specifically intended to, the amended decision is valid, provided the members had the authority to amend in the first instance. Organizational memory is not perfect; therefore, recent decisions, properly made, take precedence over previous decision when in conflict. See table 4.6 for a summary.

Table 4.6.   Amend a Previous Decision

Characteristic	Required	Further Explanation
Second	Yes	Amend a previous decision is a main motion, therefore requires a second.
Debatable	Yes	Fully debatable and may go into all aspects of the previous decision being amended.
Amendable	Yes	As *amend a previous decision* is a main motion it may be amended by primary and secondary amendments. Even if the vote required to adopt is a supermajority (see below), the primary or secondary amendments only require a majority vote.
Vote Required	Same vote as originally required	Requires the same vote as the original motion, which would normally be a majority vote. If the original motion required a supermajority vote to adopt, amending the previous decision requires the same supermajority vote. If notice was required to adopt the original motion, the same notice is again required.
May Interrupt	No	A main motion has the lowest order of precedence and may be made only when no motion is pending.
May Be Renewed	No	Amend a previous decision being a main motion is not renewable within the same meeting after it has been disposed of. It may, however, be reconsidered.
May Be Reconsidered	Yes	Both a negative and an affirmative vote may be reconsidered.

Procedure and Examples

After being recognized by the presiding officer to speak, the member says:

"I move we amend the previous decision regarding the setting of the date of the banquet by striking out 'July 6' and inserting 'July 27.'"

Or,

"I move that we amend the bylaws by striking out the second sentence of article 5.6 so that the article reads . . ."

Or,

"I move to amend the policy regarding employee parking fees by substituting the existing wording in the policy manual with . . ."

Table 4.7 summarizes the precedence of motions to amend a previous decision.

Other Considerations

Organizations often adopt policies or make decisions when a decision or policy on the subject already exists but is generally unknown. When this occurs the organization has amended or rescinded the previous decision or policy "by implication." It is not reasonable to assume that old policy or decisions are generally known or accessible to the current administration or members. If the concept of rescinding by implication were not allowed, significant problems could arise in the organization. To avoid such problems it is good practice to record all substantive decisions or policies that sustain the ongoing operation of the organization in a document of authority or policy manual. This record supports the organizational memory of the organization. Decisions that are not ongoing but are executed once need only be documented in the minutes.

Amending the bylaws is a special instance of the motion to amend a previous decision. The rules for amending the bylaws should be stated in the bylaws themselves. If the bylaws are silent and this book is the parliamentary authority, a majority vote is required to amend, provided notice has been give at the immediately previous meeting or in the regular call to the meeting.

Main Motion—Rescind a Previous Decision

A motion to *rescind a previous decision* is a main motion. It is a special case of the more general motion to amend a previous decision. Procedurally

Table 4.7. Precedence Table (Amend a Previous Decision)

Takes Precedence Over:	Yields To:
No other motion. May be made only when no other motion is pending.	All other motions, except another main motion.

and substantively there is no difference between the motions. In effect, the motion to rescind is a motion to amend a previous decision by striking out the decision altogether. If the motion is adopted, the previous decision is no longer in effect. Again, if the previous decision has been partially executed, adoption of a motion to rescind does not nullify or affect in any way action that has already been carried out. See "Amend a Previous Decision" for the rules that apply to "Rescind a Previous Decision."

After being recognized by the presiding officer to speak, the member says:

"I move we rescind the decision made at the January meeting regarding the policy on permitting guests at our meeting to speak."

Or,

"I move we amend the bylaws by striking out in its entirety Article 11."

Main Motion—Reconsider a Vote

A motion to *reconsider a vote* is a main motion. It permits an assembly to consider reversing a decision it has made at that meeting. The previous decision must have been made through a main motion. Unlike motions to ratify, rescind, or amend a previous action—which, as soon as made, restore a decision to the control of the meeting—the motion to reconsider restores the decision to the control of the meeting only if it is adopted. If the motion to reconsider is defeated, the assembly has decided not to consider reversing the previous decision. If adopted, it temporarily nullifies the previous decision and places the meeting back at the point prior to taking the vote on the original motion. The main motion originally voted on is once again pending; procedurally, it is considered a newly made main motion. All rights of the members are renewed with regard to debate. The motion may be amended, amendments previously lost may again be made, and amendments previously adopted may be reversed. All other motions are also in order.

The motion to reconsider may be made by any member of the assembly, although this right may be abused—the presiding officer may rule the making of the motion to reconsider "dilatory." The presiding officer should not make this ruling lightly but should exercise sound judgment. If the motion was adopted with little opposition and there is no new information, or the member habitually makes such motions the presiding officer may consider ruling the motion dilatory. That ruling may be appealed, in which case the assembly decides whether the motion to reconsider is in order. See table 4.8.

Procedure and Example

After being recognized by the presiding officer to speak, the member says:

1. "I move to reconsider the vote made earlier in the meeting regarding the expenses of the treasurer."
2. After a second, the presiding officer says, "It is moved and seconded that we reconsider the vote on the expenses of the treasurer, which

Table 4.8. Reconsider a Vote

Characteristic	Required	Further Explanation
Second	Yes	Reconsider a Vote is a main motion therefore requires a second.
Debatable	Yes	Debate may only go into the reasons for reconsidering.
Amendable	No	There are no variables to be amended in the motion to Reconsider a Vote.
Vote Required	Majority	Even if the underlying motion required a supermajority to adopt, the motion to reconsider that motion only requires a majority vote.
May Interrupt	Yes	The making of the motion to reconsider may interrupt proceedings but not a speaker. If the motion to reconsider cannot be taken up at the time of the making of the motion to reconsider, the interruption, in effect, gives notice to the assembly that the motion to reconsider will be taken up at an appropriate time later in the meeting.
May Be Renewed	No	Because the motion to reconsider is a main motion, it is not renewable with essentially the same main motion.
May Be Reconsidered	No	It is not logical to reconsider a motion to reconsider.

was defeated. Discussion may address only the merits of reconsidering or not reconsidering this decision. Is there any discussion?"

3. After discussion the presiding officer says, "Shall the assembly reconsider the vote on the expenses of the treasurer, which was earlier defeated?"

4. If the motion to reconsider is defeated, the meeting continues to the next business.

5. If the motion to reconsider is adopted, the presiding officer states the motion as originally defeated—for example, "The motion to reconsider the vote has been adopted. The motion before you is that the treasurer receive one hundred dollars per month in lieu of expenses. All rights of debate and amendment are restored on this motion. Is there any discussion?"

Table 4.9 summarizes the precedence of motions to reconsider a vote.

Other Considerations

The motion to reconsider is often confusing to members. The presiding officer must carefully explain each step of the process to the assembly. The presiding officer should be well rehearsed in the steps involved in reconsidering a vote.

A further complication is that a motion to reconsider might be made when the assembly is not in a position to take it up. For example, during the consideration of the bylaws a member may move to reconsider a main motion that was considered under committee

Table 4.9. Precedence Table (Reconsider a Vote)

Takes Precedence Over:	Yields To:
No other motion. Is normally made when no motion is pending but has the unique feature that it may interrupt proceedings but not a speaker to state the motion.	The motion to postpone, limit, extend or close debate, postpone temporarily, and all privileged and incidental motions truly incidental to the meeting situation.
	Does not yield to another main motion, amend, or refer to a committee.

reports earlier in the meeting. If the motion receives a second, the presiding officer states that the motion to reconsider will be taken up later in the meeting. This gives, in effect, notice of the motion to reconsider. At the appropriate time, the presiding officer or any member may call up the motion to reconsider. The motion must be taken up before the meeting concludes, as it would lose effect at adjournment.

The presiding officer has a degree of discretion, however, as to when the motion to reconsider should be called up. For example, using the earlier example, if a bylaw change has made a previous decision in the meeting nonsensical, it may be appropriate to take up the motion to reconsider a previous decision during the bylaws. The presiding officer makes this decision, which may be appealed.

The motion to reconsider affords the assembly broad latitude to make a different decision. However, because, as noted, it is open to abuse, it must be carefully controlled by the presiding officer and the assembly in general. A motion to reconsider is best made when no other motion is pending.

Main Motion—To Remove a Decision From a Committee

A motion to *remove a decision from a committee* is a main motion. It permits an assembly to consider and vote on a motion or a particular subject that is properly under the jurisdiction of a committee. To remove a decision from a committee, the assembly must have the authority in the first instance to make the decision. If a committee fails to report, an emergency arises that requires a quicker decision, or it is otherwise in the best interest of the organization to deal with the subject immediately, this motion may be used. See table 4.10.

Unlike motions to ratify, rescind, or amend a previous action, which in themselves restore a decision to the control of the assembly, a motion to remove a decision from a committee restores the decision to the control of the assembly only on its adoption. If the motion to remove a decision from a committee fails, the committee continues to own the decision. If adopted, the motion is now owned by the assembly; the presiding officer immediately places it before the assembly, unless the motion to remove was qualified as to when the underlying motion or

Table 4.10.   Remove a Decision from a Committee

Characteristic	Required	Further Explanation
Second	Yes	Remove a Decision from a Committee is a main motion, therefore requires a second.
Debatable	Yes	Debate may only go into the merits of returning the decision to the superior body.
Amendable	Yes	May be amended only with regard to the time when the motion or subject being removed from the committee may be considered.
Vote Required	Majority	Even if the underlying motion or decision requires a supermajority, the vote to remove the decision from a committee requires only a majority.
May Interrupt	No	This motion is a main motion and may be made only when no motion is pending.
May Be Renewed	Yes	May be renewed after progress has been made in the discussion or meeting.
May Be Reconsidered	No	The motion may not be reconsidered but a negative vote on the motion to Remove a Decision from a Committee may be renewed. In addition, referring the motion again to the committee may reverse an affirmative vote on the motion to Remove a Decision from a Committee.

subject is to be considered. If what has been removed from a committee is a subject, as opposed to a definitive motion, the presiding officer states the subject and permits informal consideration until a member makes a motion.

The motion to remove a decision from a committee may be applied to a motion, decision, or subject area of any committee, standing or special, of an organization. Although a standing committee has jurisdiction over a certain subject area, unless that committee has the specific power to act in a given instance, a decision may be removed by the board and dealt with. For example, if a committee has the specific power to impose a penalty in a discipline case, such a decision may not be removed from the committee. In such instances the presiding officer should rule the motion to remove a decision from a committee out of order.

Procedure and Example

After being recognized by the presiding officer to speak, the member says:

1. "I move to remove the decision regarding the construction of a bicycle path from the building committee and place it before this meeting for consideration."
2. After a second, the presiding officer says, "It has been moved and seconded that we remove the decision regarding the bicycle path from the building committee and place it before this meeting. Discussion may address only the merits of removing the decision from the building committee. Is there any discussion?"
3. After discussion the presiding officer says, "Shall the assembly remove the decision regarding the construction of a bicycle path from the building committee and place it before this meeting?"
4. If the motion to remove the decision from the committee is defeated, the assembly continues to the next business.
5. If the motion to remove the decision from the committee is adopted, the presiding officer states the motion as originally referred to the committee. For example, "The motion to remove the decision from the committee has been adopted. The motion before you is that five hundred thousand dollars be allocated to the building fund budget to construct a bicycle path between Newton Road and Maxwell Avenue. All rights of debate and amendment are restored to the members on this motion. Is there any discussion?"

Table 4.11 summarizes the precedence of motions to remove a decision from a committee.

Other Considerations

It is good organizational practice to allocate jurisdiction for certain organizational needs to various committees. This is normally done through standing committees, defined in the documents of authority.

Table 4.11. Precedence Table (Remove a Decision from a Committee)

Takes Precedence Over:	Yields To:
No other motion. May be made only when no other motion is pending.	The motions to amend, postpone, limit, extend, or close debate, postpone temporarily, and all privileged and incidental motions truly incidental to the meeting situation.
	Does not yield to another main motion, or refer to a committee.

Special committees are used for business that does not readily belong in the mandate of a standing committee. The board of the organization normally maintains overall jurisdiction and authority for decisions. However, in some cases a committee is given the power to act without referring the decision to the board. In these instances, the board does not have authority in the first instance to make the decision; the committee does.

Main Motions—Ratify and Confirm

The motions to *ratify* and *confirm* are main motions. They formally bring substantive proposals before the meeting for decision by the members.

The motion to ratify approves or sanctions the act of an officer, board, inquorate meeting, or any other entity of the organization that, without authority, took emergency action.

The motion to confirm permits a superior body to assent formally to any action of a subordinate body, when requested by that body or when required by the documents of authority.

Motions to ratify and confirm are dealt with identically. Once the motion to ratify or confirm has been stated by the presiding officer, the original motion is pending. See table 4.12.

Table 4.12. Ratify or Confirm

Characteristic	Required	Further Explanation
Second	Yes	The motions to *Ratify* and *Confirm* are main motions and require a second.
Debatable	Yes	Is fully debatable and may go into all aspects of the question being ratified or confirmed.
Amendable	Yes	Amendments must be germane to the original motion being ratified or confirmed. The original motion or part of the motion is not amendable if the original motion or part of it has been acted on.
Vote Required	Majority	A main motion normally requires a majority vote to adopt. If the original motion being ratified or confirmed required a supermajority to adopt the ratification or confirmation must also adopt with the same supermajority.
May Interrupt	No	The motions to *Ratify* and *Confirm* are main motions and have the lowest order of precedence and may be made only when no motion is pending.
May Be Renewed	No	These motions are main motions and are not renewable within the same meeting after they have been disposed of. They may be reconsidered.
May Be Reconsidered	Yes	Both a negative and an affirmative vote may be reconsidered.

Procedure and Example

After being recognized by the presiding officer to speak, the member says:

1. "I move that we ratify the decision by the president to travel to Seattle at an expense to the organization of $1,200."
   After a member seconds the motion, the presiding officer states the motion, asks for discussion, and in due time takes the vote. If the motion is defeated, the organization will not pay for the president's trip.
2. "I move that the board confirm the decision of the building committee in the stance that it is taking in its negotiations with the city regarding our new headquarters."

Table 4.13   Precedence Table (Ratify and Confirm)

Takes Precedence Over:	Yields To:
No other motion. May be made only when no other motion is pending.	All other motions, except another main motion.

It is assumed that the building committee has power to act in the negotiations but wishes to put on record the full support of the board in its position.

Table 4.13 summarizes precedence for motions to ratify and confirm.

Other Considerations

Motions to ratify and confirm are similar in intent and are often used interchangeably. A motion to ratify asks for retroactive approval of an act done without authority, while a motion to confirm asks for an expression of agreement with an act proposed to be done, *with* authority. It is often useful for a lower body to request of a superior body confirmation of a decision before executing the decision, but the subordinate body takes the chance that its decision will be amended or even rejected.

The major difference between ratify and confirm is that the action under ratify has been taken, while that under confirm is still to be taken.

Because of the nature of a motion to ratify and confirm, its exact wording is often known ahead of time and should be included in the call of the meeting.

When a committee makes a recommendation in the form of a motion, it is not appropriate merely to ratify or confirm it; the committee should present the original motion in full to the meeting.

CHAPTER FIVE

~

Motion to Amend

A motion to *amend* proposes a formal change to the pending motion. The purpose of an amendment is to make the motion acceptable to more members.

The motion to amend is applicable to any motion that contains words, numbers, dates, or clauses that may be varied. It is not used to change one type of motion into another type. For example, it is not used to change the motion to recess to a motion to adjourn by striking out "recess" and inserting "adjourn."

There are four forms of amendment:

- Amend by inserting a word or words

- Amend by striking out a word or words

- Amend by striking out a word or words and inserting a word or words

- Amend by substituting

Whichever form is used, the amendment must be germane to the motion to which it is being applied. An amendment must not introduce a new subject. For example, if the main motion were "That we insure the building for $200,000," an amendment that added the words, "and that we rent the top floor" would not be germane. The presiding officer would rule the amendment out of order, stating that it is not germane to insuring the building. The member could appeal this ruling, or the presiding officer, if unsure of the relevance of the amendment, could ask the assembly to decide.

When an amendment is applied to a motion, it is called a *primary* amendment. When applied to another amendment, it is called a *secondary* amendment. A secondary amendment is sometimes called an "amendment to an amendment." A secondary amendment may not have a third amendment applied to it. See table 5.1 for characteristics of a motion to amend.

Table 5.1. Motion to Amend

Characteristic	Required	Further Explanation
Second	Yes	All amendments require a second.
Debatable	Yes	An amendment is debatable if the motion to which it is applied is debatable. Debate may not go into the merits of the motion being amended.
Amendable	Yes	A primary amendment is amendable, but a secondary amendment is not amendable.
Vote Required	Majority	An amendment never requires more than a majority vote, even if the motion being amended requires a supermajority vote.
May Interrupt	No	
May Be Renewed	Yes/No	An amendment is not normally renewable. However, if the motion has been substantially changed, renewing an amendment may be initiated at the discretion of the presiding officer or assembly when main motion is pending.
May Be Reconsidered	No	An amendment may be renewed in certain circumstances (see above). A motion to *amend a previous action* may also be used.

Procedure and Examples

Amending the Main Motion

Assume the following main motion is pending: "That the association develop a five year plan and that we hire a consultant to develop the plan." The following motions to amend would be in order:

Amend by Inserting a Word or Words
"I move that we add the word, 'financial' before the word 'plan'"
Or,
"I move that we add the words 'to increase membership' after the word 'plan.'"

Amend by Striking Out a Word or Words
"I move that we strike out the words 'and that we hire a consultant to develop the plan.'"

Amend by Striking Out a Word or Words and Inserting a Word or Words
"I move that we strike out the word 'five' and insert the word 'three.'"
Or,
"I move that we strike out 'five year' and insert the words 'three year membership retention.'"

Amend by Substituting
"I move that we substitute the existing motion and replace it with the following, 'That the association hire CMS Consulting Ltd. to look into all aspects of the association's operating environment, including finances, membership, staffing and program development.'"

Amending Other Motions
Motions may be made to amend motions other than main motions, or to amend previous amendments. Examples are:

Motion to Refer
Motion: "That the main motion be referred to a committee of three appointed by the president."
Amendment: "I move to amend by striking out the words 'a committee of three appointed by the president' and insert 'the membership committee.'"

Motion to Postpone
Motion: "That the motion be postponed until 8:30 this evening."
Amendment: "I move to amend by adding the words, 'or until the treasurer arrives, whichever is earlier.'"

Motion to Fix the Time to Continue the Meeting

Motion: "To fix next Monday at 8 P.M. as the time to continue the meeting."

Amendment: "I move to strike out 'Monday' and insert 'Tuesday.'"

Primary Motion to Amend

Primary amendment: "That the motion be amended by adding the words "no later than the June meeting."

Amendment (to the amendment): I move to strike out the word 'June' and insert the word 'May.'"

When handling this latter motion, which is a secondary amendment, the presiding officer disposes of the motions in the reverse order in which they were made. In this case the motions were made as (1) a main motion, (2) an amendment, (3) an amendment to the amendment. The presiding officer would take (3) first, then (2), and having disposed of the amendments, take (1), the main motion. The main motion, of course, may have been amended, but it is always important that the main motion be voted on, no matter whether amended or not.

The above statement regarding the disposition of a series of pending motions is generally true—motions are disposed of in the reverse order in which they were made. Table 5.2 indicates the precedence of a motion to amend.

Table 5.2. Precedence Table (Amend)

Takes Precedence Over:	Yields To:
The motion to which it applies. It applies to main motions, primary amendments, refer, postpone, limit or extend debate, recess and fix the time to which to continue the meeting.	All subsidiary or privileged motions that would be in order if the subsidiary or privileged motion were being applied to the motion being amended. It also yields to incidental motions provided they are truly incidental to the meeting situation at that time.

Other Considerations

Before stating a motion, the presiding officer ensures that if adopted it will be logical and not nonsensical, and not potentially confusing. It is a rule that the presiding officer may insist that a motion be presented in writing. It is particularly important that amendments to main motions be in writing, as it may be difficult otherwise to determine if the resultant main motion would be nonsensical or confusing.

Another complication arises when an amendment to the amendment is moved. This is best illustrated through an example. If an amendment (primary) strikes out a number of words in a main motion and an amendment to the amendment (secondary) strikes out the words in the primary amendment, in essence the intention is to let stand those words in the main motion. For example, consider the following:

1. A motion to refer is made: "That the finance committee be made up of Joseph, Robert, Cassie, Kay, Timothy, Catherine, and Mariko."
2. An amendment (primary) to the motion to refer is made: "Strike out the words 'Robert, Cassie, Kay' and insert the words 'Charles, Anna.'"
3. A member now makes a motion to amend the amendment by striking out the words "Cassie, Kay."
4. If the secondary amendment passes, Cassie and Kay will remain in the main motion whether the primary amendment is adopted or defeated.

Amendments are among the most common motions made in meetings. They can also be the most confusing. The presiding officer must stay on top of the situation and handle each amendment carefully.

CHAPTER SIX

~

Delaying Motions

At times, and for various reasons, an assembly may wish to delay the making of a decision. The assembly may not have enough information to make a proper decision, or the time may not be propitious to make a decision, or time may have run out for fruitful discussion, leaving no option but to delay the decision.

There are four motions in parliamentary law that permit delay. The motions are given in table 6.1, in order of the length of time the decision is delayed.

Table 6.1 shows that the order of precedence correlates with the time delay allowed by the motion. The longer the delay, the lower the precedence (see chapter 4).

Postpone Indefinitely

The purpose of the motion to *postpone indefinitely* is to avoid making a decision on a main motion by delaying the decision to an indeterminate time beyond the current meeting. Proposals are sometimes made that it is in the best interest of the organization not to decide, whether for or against. The motion to postpone indefinitely allows the meeting to not take a position one way or the other and in effect puts the proposal into limbo until at least the next meeting. A conscious effort

Table 6.1. Precedence Table (Delaying Motions)

Motion	Length of Time	Precedence
Postpone Indefinitely	Indeterminate Time	12
Refer to a Committee	Not beyond one year	10
Postpone to a Certain Time	Not beyond three months	9
Postpone Temporarily	Not beyond current meeting	6

must be made at a future meeting to bring the proposal forward again; it is not brought up automatically. See table 6.2.

Procedure and Example

After being recognized by the president to speak, the member says, "I move to postpone indefinitely the pending motion regarding the suspension of Mr. Bernoulli." A second is given.

The president replies, "It has been moved and seconded to postpone indefinitely the motion regarding the suspension of Mr. Bernoulli. Is there any discussion?" Discussion follows, at the end of which the pres-

Table 6.2. Postpone Indefinitely

Characteristic	Required	Further Explanation
Second	Yes	
Debatable	Yes	Debate may go into only the reasons why the motion should or should not be dealt with at this time. It may go into the merits of the underlying main motion but only in respect to delaying the decision.
Amendable	No	There are no variables in the motion to *postpone indefinitely.*
Vote Required	Majority	
May Interrupt	No	
May Be Renewed	Yes	May be renewed after a negative vote on the motion, provided some progress in debate has been made.
May Be Reconsidered	No	May be renewed after a negative vote (see above). The motion postponed indefinitely may be made again at a subsequent meeting.

ident declares, "The motion before you is to postpone indefinitely the motion regarding the suspension of Mr. Bernoulli. All those in favor of postponing indefinitely the motion say 'aye' [pause]. All those opposed to postponing indefinitely say 'no.' The ayes [noes] have it, and the motion has [has not] been postponed indefinitely."

If the motion to postpone indefinitely is adopted, the matter may not be brought back at the same meeting. If the motion to postpone indefinitely is defeated, discussion on the main motion continues. However, the motion to postpone indefinitely may be itself renewed after discussion has progressed. If the motion is renewed a second time, the presiding officer may consider ruling the motion out of order, or a member may bring the apparent abuse to the attention of the meeting, thereby forcing a ruling.

Precedence for a motion to postpone indefinitely is given in table 6.3.

Other Considerations

Motions to postpone indefinitely are not often proposed, mainly because the need for an organization to avoid taking a position on a subject, one way or another, does not arise often. It is also more satisfying and simple to say yes or no to a proposal. But when occasions do arise when it is in the interest of the organization not to take a position, the objective can be accomplished by postponing to the next meeting or sending the matter to a committee so as to delay the decision. However, both of these options, if properly followed, will eventually bring the subject back to the assembly; "postpone indefinitely" does not.

The motion to postpone indefinitely may also be used by the opponents of a motion to gauge the support for their position through a vote. If the motion passes, they have met their objective of removing the proposal. If the motion fails, they have other options by which to attempt to defeat or delay the motion.

Table 6.3.   Precedence Table (Postpone Indefinitely)

Takes Precedence Over:	Yields To:
An original main motion	All other motions, except a main motion.

Refer to a Committee

The purpose of *referring a motion or a subject to a committee* is to make more efficient use of the organization's resources by sending a matter to a smaller group. In addition, members may be appointed to that group who are interested and have experience in the subject area and are therefore likely to provide high-quality information and recommendations to the organization.

Sometimes members propose ideas that have not been fleshed out sufficiently; the meeting may refer the idea (or subject) to a committee for a more detailed examination and a look at options. The meeting may not have enough information to make a decision on a pending main motion; in this case the main motion and any attached amendments may be referred to a committee. See table 6.4.

There are four main elements to be considered in the motion to refer. These are:

Table 6.4. Refer to a Committee

Characteristic	Required	Further Explanation
Second	Yes	
Debatable	Yes	Debate may go into only the reasons why the motion should or should not be referred to a committee. It may go into the merits of the underlying main motion but only in respect to referring the decision.
Amendable	Yes	Amendments may be made to clarify the subject being referred, who appoints the committee, the number and composition of the committee, the reporting date, and instructions to the committee.
Vote Required	Majority	
May Interrupt	No	
May Be Renewed	Yes	May be renewed if progress has been made in debate.
May Be Reconsidered	No	If the motion to refer is defeated it may be renewed (see above). If adopted, the motion to *remove a decision from a committee* may be used.

1. The mandate provided to the committee
2. The standing committee or the special committee to which the subject or motion is referred
3. When the committee is to report
4. The instructions the committee is given to carry out its mandate.

While all the above elements are important, without a clear written mandate laying out the scope of its work the committee will be unable to function effectively and at best will be inefficient.

A committee is more often formed to advise and recommend action to a superior body or the appointing body. However, a committee may be given power to act. In practice this means that the committee need not report to its appointing body but may execute decisions it makes. For example, a social committee may be given the power to hire the entertainment for quarterly meetings. Discipline committees are often given mandates to hold trials, find members guilty or not guilty as charged, and set penalties as required. Such powers would be defined in the organization's document of authority, usually the bylaws.

When referring a motion to a committee the assembly may make the referral to a standing committee or a special committee. Standing committees are established to deal with subjects in which the organization has an ongoing interest. Often bylaws provide that all referrals of certain subjects be to a particular standing committee. From time to time, however, it may be necessary to establish a special committee to examine a subject or recommend disposition of a main motion. The motion to refer does not need to include the number of members on the committee or the appointment method. However, if the motion to refer passes, the presiding officer must immediately deal with the composition of the committee. If the documents of authority are silent on appointment of members to committees, any member may propose them through a motion.

The most common method of appointing members to special committees is to provide in the documents of authority that the president has the authority to appoint all committee chairs and members. Some organizations require ratification of all appointments by the board, no matter who appoints the chair or the members to committees. Table 6.5 shows some of the common methods of appointing committees.

Table 6.5. Common Methods of Appointing Committees

Appointment of Chair By:	Appointment of Committee Members By:	Ratification By:
Motion	Motion	Not applicable
President	President	Board
President	Chair of Committee	Board
Board	Board	Not applicable
Election	Election	Not applicable
Election	Committee	Not applicable

If the president has the authority to appoint members to a committee but the appointments require ratification, the ratifying body (usually the board) may not add new names to the committee. If an appointment is not ratified, the president appoints another member and presents the new name for ratification.

If a motion to refer is used to appoint committee members, the first-named member is the chair, unless the motion identifies another person as chair.

Since it is generally advisable that the chair have the confidence of the other members, the committee may be granted authority to select its own chair.

Procedure and Example

1. After recognition by the presiding officer to speak, a member says, "I move that the subject of acquiring a second mortgage on our building be referred to the finance committee, that the committee be instructed to consult with our bank manager regarding financial options, and that the committee report at our June meeting." The above motion is a main motion that refers a subject to committee, with no other motion pending.

2. "I move that the pending motion regarding a second mortgage, with the attached amendments, be referred to the finance committee to report at the next meeting." This motion refers a main motion and its amendments to a committee.

3. "I move that the pending motion regarding the upcoming civic celebrations be referred to a committee of three, to be appointed by the president, and to report at the next meeting. Further that

the committee be instructed to consult with the mayor's committee on all details of the celebrations and how our organization may best help." This example refers a motion to a special committee, to be appointed by the president, with reporting requirements and instructions. It contains all the elements of a motion to refer.

4. "I move that a committee of five, with Mr. Maxwell as chair, and Ms. Todd, Ms. Cornwall, Mr. Piper, and Mr. Coates as members, investigate the type of halls available for our biennial banquet and that they be given the power to contract for the use of a hall, provided the cost does not exceed $1,500 for the day." This motion gives the special committee power to act but restricts that power. It also lists the members.

The following additional example provides for the striking of a special committee and its subsequent reporting. The example shows that notwithstanding the recommendation of the committee, the pending motion that was referred to the committee remains unchanged, and is so stated by the presiding officer. Assume that the following main motion and amendment are pending:

Main motion: That the association appoint two members to the university faculty committee to represent the interests of the association in research matters.

Amendment: To strike out the word "two" and insert "one."

A member now makes the following motion, which is adopted: "That the main motion and attached amendment be referred to a committee of three to be appointed by the president and that they report at the next meeting."

The committee reports its finding and conclusions at the next meeting, proposing "that the amendment and the main motion be defeated." The presiding officer replies, "Notwithstanding the recommendation of the special committee, the motion before you is on the amendment to strike out the word 'two' and insert the word 'one.'"

That is, the presiding officer takes up the business at the point at which it was referred to the committee, this time with the benefit of the analysis of the special committee and its recommendations. The motion to amend is dealt with, then the main motion.

Precedence for a motion to refer to a committee is given in table 6.6.

Table 6.6.   Precedence Table (Refer to a Committee)

Takes Precedence Over:	Yields To:
Main motions Postpone Indefinitely Amendments to the main motion	All other motions

Other Considerations

An organization should maintain a journal listing the attributes of all its committees, including current members, current plans, and assigned duties and responsibilities. This book would have the following entries:

1. Committee name
2. Type of committee
3. Committee mandate and objectives
4. Where the committee derives its authority
5. Number of members on committee
6. How members and chair are appointed
7. Term of office of members and chair
8. Quorum required to conduct business
9. Committee's reporting requirement.

This data would be augmented with current committee information:

10. Name of chair and members
11. Meeting dates
12. Committee plans
13. List of business referred to the committee
14. Minutes of meetings.

An individual committee, depending on its nature, may maintain a separate committee book. This provides a historical account of the committees of the organization, which is especially useful for those that continue from year to year.

See appendix C for a typical committee journal.

Postpone to a Certain Time

The purpose of the motion to *postpone to a certain time* is to permit the assembly to delay a decision, usually because of time pressure or because insufficient information is available. See table 6.7.

The motion to postpone may delay an item of business as follows:

* To a time within the current meeting

* To the next meeting, provided the meeting is held before the end of the third month following.

If an assembly wishes to postpone a motion beyond three months, it should refer the motion to a committee. If the assembly expects to delay decisions beyond three months regularly, it should adopt a special rule to that effect.

Table 6.7. Postpone to a Certain Time

Characteristic	Required	Further Explanation
Second	Yes	
Debatable	Yes	Debate may go into only the reasons why the motion should or should not be postponed. Debate may go into the merits of the underlying motion but only in respect to postponing.
Amendable	Yes	Amendments may be made to the time of postponement and to making the postponement a special order.
Vote Required	Majority	No matter the form of the motion, including the motion as a special order, the vote required is a majority.
May Interrupt	No	
May Be Renewed	Yes	May be renewed if progress has been made in debate.
May Be Reconsidered	No	If defeated the motion to postpone may be renewed (see above). If adopted, a motion to suspend the rules to consider the business postponed may be moved (similar to changing the agenda).

The motion to postpone may specify a general time, a specific time, or an event. For example, a motion may be made "to postpone the pending motion until new business." Another example, showing a specific time: "I move to postpone the motion until 9 P.M. this evening." When 9 P.M. arrives the pending business is completed, and the postponed business is taken up.

The motion to postpone may also be presented as a special order. An example is, "I move to postpone the main motion until 9:30 A.M. tomorrow and to make it a special order." The effect here is that whatever business is pending at 9:30 A.M. must be set aside and the special order taken up, unless a vote is in progress, in which case the vote is completed.

A motion to postpone that is adopted takes with it all motions that then adhere to the original main motion.

Procedure and Examples

Assume the following main motion is pending: "that the association appoint a committee of three to visit the four new sporting facilities that have recently been built in the city."

A member may make any of the following motions:

1. "That the main motion be postponed until our meeting in June." Provided the current meeting is taking place in March, April, or May, the motion is in order. If the motion read "July" and the current meeting was in March, the presiding officer would rule the motion out of order.
2. "That the motion be postponed until 3 P.M. tomorrow or until the sports director arrives at the meeting, whichever is earlier."
3. "That the motion be postponed until our meeting next month and made a special order for 7:15 P.M."
4. "That the motion be postponed until the president arrives." In this example, a member may move a motion to amend: "I move to amend the motion to postpone by adding the words, 'and to make the motion a special order for that time.'" If this amendment is adopted and the motion to postpone is adopted, the taking up of the motion has been made a special order; the main motion must be considered as soon as the president arrives.

Precedence for *postpone to a certain time* is given in table 6.8.

Table 6.8. Precedence Table (Postpone to a Certain Time)

Takes Precedence Over:	Yields To:
Main motion	All other motions
Postpone Indefinitely	
Refer to a committee	
Amendments to the above motions	

Other Considerations:

The purpose of limiting the motion to postpone to three months is to avoid its being used to kill main motions. Postponement also effectively takes it out of the hands of the assembly for the time of the postponement. If the assembly wishes to consider a motion that has been postponed, it may do so by a motion to rescind the postponement.

Postpone Temporarily

The purpose of the motion to *postpone temporarily* is to set aside business for a short period of time, but no later than the end of the meeting. It is used when an interruption in the meeting makes it expedient not to continue with the business at that time.

The presiding officer often assumes the motion. For example, if a tellers committee returns with election results, the presiding officer may say, "If there is no objection we will postpone the current business temporarily until the tellers committee reports [pause]. There being no objection, the business is set aside temporarily." After the tellers have reported and the election results have been dealt with, the presiding officer will say, "If there is no objection we will resume consideration of the business previously set aside [pause]. There being no objection, the business before you is . . ."

An item of business that has been postponed temporarily may be taken up again through a motion to resume consideration. The presiding officer often assumes this motion, as in the example above. However, any member of the assembly may do so (see below, "Resume Consideration"). See table 6.9.

Table 6.9. Postpone Temporarily

Characteristic	Required	Further Explanation
Second	Yes	The presiding officer often assumes the motion.
Debatable	No	It would defeat the purpose of the motion to debate it.
Amendable	No	There are no variables in the motion to *postpone temporarily*.
Vote Required	Majority	The presiding officer often assumes the motion, but if made by a member a majority adopts.
May Interrupt	No	
May Be Renewed	Yes	May be renewed if progress has been made in debate.
May Be Reconsidered	No	If defeated it may be renewed (see above). If adopted the motion to *resume consideration* may be used.

To take an example, consider a meeting with business in progress when its keynote speaker arrives. If the presiding officer fails to notice, a member gains the floor and says, "Mr. President our special speaker has arrived. I move that the pending business be postponed temporarily." Another member seconds.

The president replies, "It has been moved and seconded that we postpone the pending business temporarily. All those in favor say 'aye' [pause]. All those against say 'no.' The ayes have it, and the business is set aside temporarily."

The president could also handle the motion through general consent. Precedence for a motion to postpone temporarily is given in table 6.10.

Table 6.10. Precedence Table (Postpone Temporarily)

Takes Precedence Over:	Yields To:
Main motions Postpone Indefinitely Refer to a committee Postpone Limit or extend debate Close debate and vote immediately Amendments to the above motions	All privileged motions. It also yields to incidental motions provided they are truly incidental to the meeting situation at that time.

Resume Consideration

The purpose of the motion to *resume consideration* is to bring back business that has been set aside temporarily.

The presiding officer often assumes the motion after the interruption for which the business was set aside has been dealt with. If the presiding officer does not, any member may make the motion.

If business has been postponed temporarily in a meeting and no motion to resume consideration is made, or it is not assumed by the presiding officer before adjournment, the business falls to the floor. It may be initiated again at the next meeting through a new main motion. See table 6.11.

Procedure and Example

Member A: "Mr. President, I move that we resume consideration of the business regarding our privacy statement that was set aside temporarily this morning." Another member seconds the motion.

President: "It has been moved and seconded that we resume consideration of the business regarding our privacy statement that was set aside temporarily this morning. All those in favor say 'aye' [pause]. All

Table 6.11. Resume Consideration

Characteristic	Required	Further Explanation
Second	Yes	The presiding officer often assumes the motion.
Debatable	No	It would defeat the purpose of the motion to debate it.
Amendable	No	There are no variables in the motion to *resume consideration*.
Vote Required	Majority	The presiding officer often assumes the motion, but if made by a member a majority adopts.
May Interrupt	No	
May Be Renewed	Yes	May be renewed after progress has been made in the meeting.
May Be Reconsidered	No	If defeated it may be renewed (see above). If adopted there are no advantages to reconsidering the motion to *resume consideration*.

Table 6.12.　Precedence Table (Resume Consideration)

Takes Precedence Over:	Yields To:
No other motion. It may be made only when no other business is pending.	All privileged motions. It also yields to incidental motions, provided they are truly incidental to the meeting situation at that time.

those against say 'no.' The ayes have it, and the business before you is the motion regarding the privacy statement. The secretary will read the privacy statement motion."

The president could also have handled the motion through general consent.

Precedence for a motion to resume consideration is given in table 6.12.

Other Considerations

The adoption of the motion to resume consideration takes the assembly back to the parliamentary situation that existed when the business was set aside. Any restrictions on debate that were in effect then are again in place, and members who had exhausted their debate time may not debate unless the assembly allows them to speak again.

After business is resumed, all motions that are in order may be made, including the motion to postpone temporarily if the situation requires it.

CHAPTER SEVEN

~

Motions That Affect Debate

Members have a right to debate, but that right is not absolute. For example, this manual puts a limit on that right, allowing each member to speak twice for five minutes each on a debatable motion. There are three motions that affect debate, two that restrict the right to debate and one that extends the right. They are listed in table 7.1.

The orders of precedence for motions to limit and extend debate are the same. If "limit debate" is pending, "extend debate" is out of order, and vice versa.

Limit or Extend Debate

The purpose of these motions is to restrict or extend debate in some manner, such as by time or by number of speakers.

When a member believes that enough time has been spent in debate and that the members have enough information to make a decision, the member may make a motion to limit debate. Conversely, if a member believes that more information is required to make a decision or wishes to hear more speakers, the member may move to extend the limits of debate. The motion to extend debate, unlike the motion to limit debate, may also be applied to an individual speaker. If the speaker has exhausted all allowed time in debate, a member, including the member speaking,

Table 7.1. Motions That Affect Debate

Motion	Options	Applies To	Precedence
Limit Debate	By length of time Number of times a speaker speaks By number of speakers Until a certain time is reached	All speakers	8
Extend Debate	By length of time Number of times a speaker speaks By number of speakers Until a certain time is reached	All speakers or individual speakers	8
Close Debate	On the pending motion On a series of pending motions On all pending motions	All speakers	7

may request that the time be extended. If the request is denied, any member may make a motion to extend the speaker's time.

If a limitation on debate has been ordered and that limitation has been reached, the presiding officer must take a vote on the pending motion, unless the time is extended through a new motion.

The motions to limit or extend debate normally apply to the pending motions, but they may also be applied to motions not yet made. If a motion to limit or extend debate is made when no business is pending, it is itself a main motion. If adopted, the motion applies to future debate in the meeting. See table 7.2.

Procedure and Example
The following examples apply when a motion to limit or extend debate is made when current business is pending. These motions to limit or extend debate are therefore subsidiary motions.

1. After being recognized by the presiding officer to speak, the member says: "I move that we limit further debate on this subject to ten minutes." The above limitation applies to the whole topic under discussion.

Table 7.2. Limit and Extend Limits of Debate

Characteristic	Required	Further Explanation
Second	Yes	
Debatable	Yes	Debate is restricted to the form of limitation or extension of debate.
Amendable	Yes	Amendable as to the type of restriction or extension of debate.
Vote Required	2/3 Vote	Extending debate or limiting debate changes a rule of order affecting the rights of members of the assembly.
May Interrupt	No	
May Be Renewed	Yes	May be renewed if progress has been made in debate.
May Be Reconsidered	No	If defeated the motions to extend or limit debate may be renewed (see above). If adopted a new motion to limit or extend debate may be removed.

2. "I move that we limit debate on the amendment to two speakers for the amendment and two speakers against the amendment." This limitation, if adopted, applies only to the pending motion (an amendment).

3. "I move that we extend the limits of debate on the budget until 5 P.M., from the current limitation of 3 P.M." If the motion to extend is adopted and the budget is still under consideration at 5 P.M., all pending motions will be voted on at that time, unless further extended by motion.

4. "Madam President, I request that Mr. Michael Ryan be permitted an additional three minutes to complete his remark." The presiding officer may allow the request by saying, "If there is no objection, we will allow Mr. Ryan an additional three minutes [pause]. There being no objection, Mr. Ryan is allowed the three minutes. Mr. Ryan, you may continue." If an objection is made, any member may move to extend the limits of debate for Mr. Ryan. This requires a two-thirds vote to adopt.

The following examples show how the use of the motions to limit or extend debate may be used to limit or extend the rights of members in debate for part of the meeting or the remainder of the meeting. In these instances, the motions must be made when no motion is pending. The motions to limit or extend debate, in these circumstances, are main motions.

1. "I move that each speaker be allowed to speak only once per motion and for a maximum of two minutes." If this motion is adopted, the limitations are in effect until the end of the meeting, unless removed or amended through motion. To return to the regular limits in debate, a member need only move "to return to the regular limits in debate"; this requires a majority to adopt.
2. "I move that during the budget discussion each member be allowed to speak three times to each motion." If this motion is adopted, the members' rights are extended to speaking three times per debatable motion during consideration of the budget. The limit on the length of each speech is unchanged. When the budget discussion is concluded, the regular limits of debate are again in effect.

Precedence for motions to extend or limit debate is given below in table 7.3.

Close Debate

The purpose of the motion to *close debate* is to stop all debate on the pending motion or a series of consecutive pending motions, and to vote

Table 7.3. Precedence Table (Extend and Limit Debate)

Takes Precedence Over:	Yields To:
All debatable motions	Close debate, postpone temporarily, all privileged motions and all incidental motions provided they are truly incidental to the meeting situation at that time

immediately. The motion also stops the making of amendments on the motions affected. When a member believes that enough time has been spent in debate and that the members have enough information to make a decision, the member may make a motion to close debate.

If members have not spoken on a motion or have not spoken the number of times allowed, the motion to close debate, when adopted, removes their right to debate the motions upon which "close debate" has been ordered. Because the motion removes temporarily a right of a member, it requires a two-thirds vote to adopt.

If debate has been ordered closed, the presiding officer must immediately take the vote on the pending motion or motions. The order to close debate lapses when all votes affected have been taken, or the meeting has been adjourned, or the motion or motions affected have been referred to committee. If one of the motions affected is a motion to postpone and that motion is adopted, the order to close debate is still in effect, provided the postponement is to a time within the same meeting. See table 7.4.

Table 7.4.   Close Debate

Characteristic	Required	Further Explanation
Second	Yes	
Debatable	No	It would defeat the purpose of the motion if it were debatable.
Amendable	Yes	May be amendable as to the number of consecutive pending motions debate is being closed on. If the motion is not qualified, only the pending motion is affected if adopted.
Vote Required	2/3 Vote	Closing debate changes a rule of order affecting the rights of members of the assembly.
May Interrupt	No	
May Be Renewed	Yes	May be renewed if progress has been made in debate.
May Be Reconsidered	No	If defeated the motion to close debate may be renewed (see above).

Table 7.5. Precedence Table (Close Debate)

Takes Precedence Over:	Yields To:
Main Motions	Postpone temporarily, all
Postpone Indefinitely	privileged motions, and all
Refer	incidental motions, provided
Postpone	they are truly incidental to the
Limit or extend debate	meeting situation at that time.
Amendments to the above motions	
All other debatable motions	

If a main motion, an amendment, and a motion to refer to committee are pending, a motion to close debate, after recognition by the presiding officer, may be made as follows:

1. "I move that we close debate." This is in effect a motion to close debate on the pending motion—the motion to refer to a committee. If close debate is adopted by a two-thirds vote, the motion to refer to a committee is immediately voted on. If the motion to refer is defeated, the motion to amend is pending, and full debate is allowed on it.

2. "I move that we close debate on all pending motions except the main motion." If this motion is adopted, the motion to refer is immediately voted on. If it is adopted, no further vote is required, and the presiding officer will move to the next item on the agenda, and the order to close debate is exhausted. If the motion to refer is defeated, the motion to amend is immediately voted on. Once that vote is taken, the main motion is pending, with full rights of debate. If the motion to refer is adopted, the order to close debate is exhausted.

3. "I move that we close debate on all pending motions." If this motion is adopted, the motion to refer is immediately voted on. If the motion to refer is defeated, the motion to amend is immediately voted on, followed by a vote on the main motion. Again, if the motion to refer is adopted, the order to close debate is exhausted; when the main motion and the amendment return from committee, full debate will be in effect.

Precedence for motions to close debate is given in table 7.5.

~

CHAPTER EIGHT

Privileged Motions

Privileged motions in parliamentary law are those motions considered important enough to be dealt with immediately. They are given a high, or "privileged," priority and take precedence over the pending business—main motions, subsidiary motions, and in some instances incidental motions (see chapter 9). Privileged motions do not directly apply to the pending business but are concerned with individual members, the assembly, or the convenience of the members (recess and adjourn). There are four privileged motions. One of these four motions, the motion to raise a question of privilege, applies to both the assembly and to an individual in the meeting. Table 8.1 shows both forms of motions to raise a question of privilege.

From the table one sees that raising a question of privilege affecting the meeting has a higher priority than one affecting an individual.

The main emphasis in this chapter is on the motions' privileged status (when business is pending). However, the motions may also be moved when no business is pending.

Raise a Question of Privilege

The purpose of *raising a question of privilege* is to bring to the attention of the presiding officer and the members that a privilege of an individual or

Table 8.1. Privileged Motions—Short Descriptions and Precedence

Motion	Description	Precedence
Raise a Question of Privilege affecting an individual	Made when a member believes that a member's privileges are being impinged upon	5
Raise a Question of Privilege affecting the assembly	Made when a member believes that the privileges of the assembly as a whole are being impinged upon	4
Recess	Made when a member believes a short break in the meeting is required	3
Adjourn	Made when a member believes that the meeting should conclude	2
Fix the Time to Continue the Meeting	Made when a member believes that the meeting should be continued on another day	1

of the assembly generally is being affected adversely and to request that action be taken to rectify the situation. The question of privilege may be raised by:

• Stating the question of privilege as a request
• Stating the question of privilege as a motion

The presiding officer will rule on the admissibility of the question of privilege whether stated as a request or as a motion. The ruling of the presiding officer on admissibility of the question of privilege may be appealed.

If the question of privilege is allowed by the presiding officer or after appeal to the assembly, the decision has effectively been made that the question of privilege raised is important enough to interrupt proceedings and to be dealt with immediately. If the question of privilege was raised in the form of a request, the presiding officer deals with the substance of the request. If it was stated in the form of a motion, the assembly will decide by vote any action to be taken. This motion is a main motion, is debatable, is amendable, and may have other motions applied to it.

If a main motion is pending when the question of privilege is raised, any main motion arising out of the raising of the question of privilege takes precedence over the one that was pending. In such a case two main motions are pending at the same time—an unusual circumstance but required because of the importance and high ranking of the question of privilege. The main motion regarding the question of privilege is dealt with first.

Table 8.2 shows the characteristics of raising a question of privilege as it pertains to the "raising" aspects of the motion. When allowed, it is handled either as a request or as a main motion.

Table 8.2. Raise A Question of Privilege

Characteristic	Required	Further Explanation
Second	No	A second is not required to "raise" a question of privilege.
	Yes	If a question of privilege is allowed and was raised in the form of a main motion, the main motion requires a second.
Debatable	No	The "raising" of a question of privilege is not debatable.
	Yes	When allowed and if raised in the form of a main motion, it is debatable.
Amendable	No	The "raising" of a question of privilege is not amendable.
	Yes	When allowed and if raised in the form of a main motion, it is amendable.
Vote Required	No	The "raising" of a question of privilege is ruled on by the presiding officer.
	Yes	When allowed and if raised in the form of a main motion, it requires a majority vote.
May Interrupt	Yes	The "raising" of a question of privilege may interrupt the proceedings and, if it pertains to the remarks of a speaker, it may interrupt the speaker.
May Be Renewed	No	When the particular situation has been ruled on and dealt with it may not be renewed. If the situation changes, is aggravated or escalated, a new question of privilege may be raised.
May Be Reconsidered	No	The "raising" of a question of privilege may not be reconsidered but the presiding officer's ruling may be appealed from.
	Yes	If a main motion is used to determine the outcome of a question of privilege, the main motion may be reconsidered.

Impugning the motives of another member, speaking in derogatory terms to another member, or misquoting a member qualify as questions of privilege affecting an individual. A question of privilege in these circumstances may be raised; if the member is speaking at the time, the member may be interrupted. Any member, whether affected by the remarks or not, may raise the question of privilege.

Questions of privilege affecting the assembly include situations that may affect the safety and well-being of the assembly or organization. If the meeting place is unsafe or unhealthy, a member may raise a question of privilege affecting the assembly. The well-being of the organization may be put at risk through a resignation of an officer, an attack on the organization's integrity, or the compromise of confidential information. In these circumstances the matter may be important enough to interrupt proceedings and deal with immediately.

Let us clarify this procedure with some examples.

1. A member stands up without waiting to be recognized, interrupts a speaker, and says, "Madam President, I raise a question of privilege affecting the assembly." The member then awaits the president's instructions to proceed.

   President: "Please state your point."

   Member: "Madam President, the noise from the next room is interfering with members located at the back of the room. I request that the doors be closed."

   President: "It is noisy. Will the ushers please close the doors?"

2. A member declares, without seeking recognition, "Madam President, the member has maligned my business associates. I move that the member withdraw the remarks just made and apologize." Another member seconds the motion.

   The president, after assessing the remarks referred to, replies, "Your motion is in order. The motion before the assembly is that the member withdraw the remarks just made and apologize." The president handles this motion like any other main motion. The current business has been set aside to deal with the intemperate remarks of a member.

   The president, as an alternative to stating the motion, could have asked the member to withdraw his remarks and apologize. If the member did so, the matter would be ended. If the member refused, the president would state the motion.

Had the president ruled the motion out of order—saying, in essence, that the remarks by the other member were in order—the offended member could move to appeal the decision of the presiding officer (see chapter 9, "Incidental Motions").

3. A member declares, without waiting to be recognized, "Mr. President, I raise a point of privilege affecting the assembly."

President: "Please state your point."

Member: "The discussion currently under way involves confidential information that should be dealt with in a closed meeting."

President: "Your point is not well taken. It is not necessary to go into a closed meeting."

If the member does not appeal this ruling of the presiding officer, the matter is dropped, and the discussion continues.

The precedence table, table 8.3, relates to the "raising" of a question of privilege.

Recess

The purpose of the motion to *recess* is to take a break from a meeting, after which the members may quickly be reassembled or reassembled at a time set by the motion. If a meeting has been planned to extend over more than one day, the motion to recess may be used to set the time to carry on the next day. If the meeting was planned for one day but a need arises to continue the meeting the next day, a motion to recess

Table 8.3. Precedence Table (Raise a Question of Privilege)

Takes Precedence Over:	Yields To:
Main motions	Postpone temporarily, all
Postpone indefinitely	privileged motions, and all
Refer	incidental motions, provided
Postpone	they are truly incidental to the
Limit or extend debate	meeting situation at that time.
Amendments to the above motions	
All other debatable motions	

stipulating the time for the next day is equivalent to fixing a time to continue the meeting. In this case the meeting on the next day is a continued meeting.

If the motion to recess is made while other motions are pending, the recess, if adopted, must take place immediately and not at a future time. If the motion to recess is made when no other motion is pending, it may be used to set the time for a future recess. This is equivalent to amending the agenda. See table 8.4. To give two examples:

1. Assume that a main motion and an amendment are pending. A member may make the following motions:

   "Madam President, I move that we take a twenty-minute recess."
   Or,
   "Madam President, I move that we recess until 7:30 P.M."

   If adopted, the president immediately calls for the recess.

2. If a member makes the following motion while other motions are pending the presiding officer should rule the motion out of order: "Madam President, I move to recess for thirty minutes at 8 P.M.

Table 8.4. Recess

Characteristic	Required	Further Explanation
Second	Yes	
Debatable	Yes	Debate restricted to the length of time of the recess or to the time set for reassembly or the time set for a future recess.
Amendable	Yes	May be amendable as to the length of the recess or the time for reassembly or the time set for a future recess.
Vote Required	Majority	
May Interrupt	No	
May Be Renewed	Yes	May be renewed if progress has been made in debate.
May Be Reconsidered	No	If defeated, the motion to recess may be renewed (see above). If the motion to recess is adopted it is too late to reconsider it.

this evening." It is out of order because it does not relate to the current parliamentary situation and is not urgent; therefore it is not privileged. It may only be moved when there is no business pending. The general rule is that future recesses may be set only when no business is pending.

Table 8.5 gives the precedence of a motion to recess.

Adjourn

The purpose of the motion to *adjourn* is to conclude the meeting. Because members may not be kept unreasonably beyond the normal time of adjournment, the motion to adjourn is always privileged when made after the time set to conclude the meeting. If made before the time set to conclude, it may be made only as a main motion (not privileged).

Table 8.6 defines the rules of usage of the motion when privileged and when not privileged.

The rationale of table 8.6 is that a motion to adjourn made before the time set to conclude the meeting needs some debate to ascertain the will of the assembly regarding adjournment. It also shows that all motions to adjourn made before the time set must be made when no business is pending.

If a time has not been set to conclude the meeting, the motion to adjourn may be moved as a main motion or as a privileged motion (when other business is pending). The unprivileged motion to adjourn may be used to set a time to adjourn, thereby making the motion to adjourn privileged when that time arrives.

Table 8.5. Precedence Table (Recess)

Takes Precedence Over:	*Yields To:*
All motions except the privileged motions adjourn and fix the time for a continued meeting.	The privileged motions adjourn and fix the time for a continued meeting; also yields to incidental motions, provided they are truly incidental to the meeting situation at that time.

Table 8.6. Adjourn

Motion Characteristics	Adjourn moved after time set for concluding the meeting (privileged)	Adjourn moved before the time set for concluding the meeting (not privileged)
Made when business pending	Yes	No
Made when business not pending	Yes	Yes
Second	Yes	Yes
Debatable	No	Yes (restricted)
Amendable	Yes	Yes
Vote required	Majority	Majority
May interrupt	No	No
Renewable	Yes	Yes
Can be reconsidered	No	No

Assume that a meeting has been set to conclude at 9 P.M. It is now 8:20 P.M. The motion to adjourn is handled as follows:

1. A main motion is pending and is being discussed.
   Member: "Mr. President, I move we adjourn."
   President: "The motion to adjourn may not be moved when business is pending and we have time left in the meeting. The motion is out of order."
2. Assume there is no business pending but that there are items left on the agenda.
   Member: "Mr. President, I move we adjourn."
   President: "The motion to adjourn is in order at this time. I will point out that we have two other items on the agenda to deal with. The motion before you is to adjourn. Is there any discussion?"

   The president hears discussion on the motion and takes the vote. If the motion to adjourn is defeated, the president takes up the next item of business on the agenda. If it is adopted the president says,

Table 8.7. Precedence Table (Adjourn—When Time Set to Conclude the Meeting Has Been Reached)

Takes Precedence Over:	Yields To:
All motions except the privileged motion to fix the time for a continued meeting.	The privileged motion to fix the time for a continued meeting; also yields to incidental motions, provided they are truly incidental to the meeting situation at that time.

"The two items on the agenda will be placed on the agenda for the next meeting. This meeting is concluded."

3. Assume that the time to conclude the meeting has been reached. The motion to adjourn is handled as follows:

Member: "Mr. President, I move we adjourn."

President: "The motion to adjourn is in order at this time. The motion before you is to adjourn. All those in favor of adjourning please say 'aye' [pause]. Those against adjourning please say 'no' [pause]. The ayes [or noes] have it, and the meeting is concluded [will continue]."

Table 8.7 indicates the precedence of a motion to adjourn when the time previously set to conclude has been reached. Table 8.8 gives the precedence of a motion to adjourn when the time set to conclude has not been reached.

Table 8.8. Precedence Table (Adjourn—When Time Set to Conclude the Meeting Has Not Been Reached)

Takes Precedence Over:	Yields To:
No other motion. May be moved only when no business is pending.	The privileged motion to fix the time for a continued meeting; also yields to incidental motions, provided they are truly incidental to the meeting situation at that time.

Fix the Time for a Continued Meeting

The purpose of the motion to *fix the time for a continued meeting* is to set the time and date when the assembly will reconvene to continue its business after the current meeting is adjourned. The time set may not go beyond the next regular meeting or, if a special meeting has been scheduled, beyond the date of that meeting.

The motion is always privileged, whether business is pending or not. The motion has the highest privilege of all motions and may even be made after the motion to adjourn has been made and voted on, provided the presiding officer has not stated that the meeting is concluded. See table 8.9.

Let us consider an example:

Member: "Madam President, I move that we set next Wednesday at 3 P.M. as the time to continue this meeting." A second is made.

President: "It has been moved and seconded to set the time to continue this meeting next Wednesday at 3 P.M. Is there any discussion?"

Limited discussion is allowed, and a member may move to amend the date and time of the meeting. Whether the motion to fix the time for the continued meeting is adopted or defeated, the president now takes up the next item of business in the current meeting. Fix-

Table 8.9.　Fix the Time for a Continued Meeting

Characteristic	Required	Further Explanation
Second	Yes	
Debatable	Yes	Debate restricted to time and date of the continued meeting.
Amendable	Yes	May be amendable as to the time and date of the continued meeting.
Vote Required	Majority	
May Interrupt	No	
May Be Renewed	Yes	May be renewed if progress has been made in debate.
May Be Reconsidered	No	If the motion to fix the time for a continued meeting is defeated, it may be renewed (see above). If the motion is adopted, the motion to rescind may be used to reverse the previous decision.

Table 8.10. Precedence Table (Fix Time for a Continued Meeting)

Takes Precedence Over:	Yields To:
All motions	Yields to incidental motions provided they are truly incidental to the meeting situation at that time.

ing the time for a continued meeting does not adjourn the current meeting.

Table 8.10 gives the precedence of a motion to fix the time for a continued meeting.

CHAPTER NINE

~

Incidental Motions

An incidental motion deals mainly with procedural aspects of the pending business or of the meeting generally. Although the motions are termed "incidental," they are very important to the integrity and efficiency of the meeting. They allow members to bring to the attention of the assembly when a rule is broken, allow the presiding officer to make rulings, and allow the assembly to overrule the presiding officer. They also allow motions to be divided, withdrawn, and revoted when necessary. See table 9.1.

Incidental motions have no inherent order of precedence. As a class, incidental motions do not break down readily into groups. However, the following table provides a categorization of incidental motions related to:

- Rules

- Information

- Efficiency

- Voting

Table 9.1. Incidental Motion Categories

Category	Incidental Motion	When the Motion is Made
Incidental Motions Relating to Rules	Point of Order	When a rule has been broken
	Appeal a Decision of the Presiding Officer	When a member believes the presiding officer has ruled incorrectly
	Suspend the Rules	When a member believes that the rules are interfering with the conduct of business
	Request to be Excused from a Duty	When a member wishes to be relieved from carrying out a duty
Incidental Motion Relating to Information	Request for Information	When a member requires additional information
Incidental Motions Relating to Efficient Meetings	Consider by Paragraph	When a member believes that considering complicated motions by paragraph may be more efficient or accurate
	Request to Withdraw a Motion	When a member wishes to withdraw a motion
Incidental Motions Relating to Voting	Division of a Question	When a member believes that dividing the question into independent motions will permit the will of the assembly to be better attained
	Doubt the Vote	When a member believes the voice vote may be inaccurate
	Physical Methods of Voting	When a member wishes to propose a way of conducting a vote different from the normal voice vote or show of hands

Incidental Motions Relating to Rules

Point of Order

The purpose of *raising a point of order* is to bring to the attention of the presiding officer and the members that a rule has been broken or an error in procedure has been made and to ask that the rules be followed or the error corrected. The point of order is to be raised immediately and the matter corrected; otherwise, the opportunity may be lost or become moot. If not brought up in a timely fashion, it may be brought up only if the breach of the rules is of a continuing nature, such as a continuing breach of a document of authority. If the member is unsure that a breach of a rule has taken place the member may "reserve" a point of order, thereby giving notice that a point of order may be made in the future when the breach is clearer or if it becomes more acute.

The presiding officer has the authority to rule on the point of order, which ruling may be appealed by any member (see below for the procedure for appealing the decision of the presiding officer). If the presiding officer declines to rule on the point of order, it falls to the assembly to decide, by majority vote. The point of order then becomes debatable, if the underlying motion upon which the point was raised is debatable. A decision by the assembly on a point of order is not appealable.

Table 9.2 shows the characteristics of the point of order when the presiding officer rules on it. The comments section of the table deals with when the assembly decides the point.

Let us consider some examples clarifying the procedure.

1. Member: "Mr. President" (awaits recognition).
   President: "The member is recognized."
   Member: "Mr. President, point of order."
   President: "Please state your point."
   Member: "The item on the agenda concerning the clubhouse roof has been skipped."
   President: "The member is correct. We will take up the agenda item regarding the clubhouse roof."
2. *Member* (without waiting for recognition): "Madam President, point of order regarding the speaker's remarks."
   President: "Please state your point and the remarks you are referring to."
   Member: "The member is speaking off topic. His remarks are not relevant to the amendment."
   President: "The member is correct, the point is well taken." Then, addressing the speaker, "The member will please keep his remarks germane to the amendment. Now please continue."

Table 9.2. Point of Order

Characteristic	Required	Further Explanation
Second	No	It requires only one member to raise a *point of order*. The presiding officer then decides the point of order or the presiding officer may turn it over to the assembly to decide by majority vote.
Debatable	No/Yes	The *point of order* is not debatable unless the assembly is to decide the point. If the assembly is to decide the point of order it may be debated, provided the motion from which the point was raised is debatable.
Amendable	No	There is nothing to amend in a *point of order*.
Vote Required	No	If decided by the presiding officer, no vote is required.
	Yes	If decided by the assembly, a majority vote is required.
May Interrupt	No/Yes	A *point of order* may not interrupt a speaker unless the rule being broken relates to the remarks of a speaker.
May Be Renewed	No/Yes	When the particular situation has been ruled on and dealt with, it may not be renewed. However, if the parliamentary situation changes, or the situation is aggravated or escalated, a new point of order may be raised.
May Be Reconsidered	No	A *point of order* when decided by the presiding officer may be appealed. If decided by the assembly it may not be appealed.

Or,

If the president does not agree that the remarks were not germane, she says:

President: "The point is not well taken. The speaker's remarks are on topic." Turning to the speaker, she says, "You may continue." If the member believes that the president is incorrect, the member may appeal the decision of the presiding officer.

A point of order raised while another point of order is pending is decided by the presiding officer, with no right of appeal. Other precedence rules for point of order are given in table 9.3.

Table 9.3. Precedence Table (Point of Order)

Takes Precedence Over:	Yields To:
All motions or situations out of which a point of order may arise	The motion to postpone temporarily and all privileged motions, provided these motions are of a higher precedence than the last ranked motion pending. It also yields to incidental motions provided they are truly incidental to the meeting situation at that time.
	If the point of order is turned over to the assembly to decide and it is debatable, the motions to limit, extend, and close debate may be applied to the point of order.

Appeal a Decision of the Presiding Officer

The purpose of the motion to *appeal a decision of the presiding officer* is to permit the assembly, by majority vote, to replace the presiding officer's decision with its own decision. The presiding officer, in the first instance, has the right to rule on breaches of the rules and on other meeting situations that may arise from time to time. However, the assembly has the final authority on all decisions. On the initiation of two members, a mover and a seconder, the assembly may exert its authority. See table 9.4.

Procedure and Examples

After the presiding officer makes a ruling, any member may appeal it. The procedure for any appeal is as follows:

1. A member may without recognition declare, "I appeal the decision of the presiding officer." Someone seconds the appeal.
2. The presiding officer replies, "The decision of the presiding officer is appealed."
3. The presiding officer then states succinctly the reason for the ruling. The presiding officer asks for discussion, in which the originator of the appeal has the right to speak first.

Table 9.4. Appeal a Decision of the Presiding Officer

Characteristic	Required	Further Explanation
Second	Yes	
Debatable	Yes	The presiding officer is permitted to state the reasons for the ruling or decision and has the right to speak first and last in debate no matter the rules of debate in effect at that time
	No	If the underlying motion to which the appeal is applied to is not debatable, then the appeal is not debatable.
Amendable	No	There is nothing to amend in an appeal.
Vote Required	Yes	The vote is taken on "sustaining the decision of the presiding officer." A 50% vote or higher is required to sustain the decision of the presiding officer. A majority vote in the negative will overturn the decision of the presiding officer.
May Interrupt	Yes	An appeal may interrupt the proceedings after the presiding officer has ruled, provided a subsequent speaker has not begun speaking.
May Be Renewed	No	The assembly's decision is final in the matter.
May Be Reconsidered	No	The assembly's decision is final in the matter.

4. When discussion is complete, the presiding officer takes the vote. The presiding officer states the motion in a positive manner: "All those in favor of sustaining the decision of the presiding officer say 'aye' [pause]. Those against sustaining the decision of the presiding officer say 'no.'"

5. The presiding officer now declares the result. The decision of the presiding officer is sustained on an aye vote of 50 percent or higher.

To take an example illustrating the above procedure:

President: "The president rules that the motion is out of order."

Member (without waiting for recognition): "Madam President, I appeal the decision of the presiding officer" (second).

President: "The decision of the presiding officer has been appealed regarding the motion made by the member. In my opinion the motion is out of order because the subject brought up by the member relates to the motion that was referred to the finance committee earlier this morning. We must await the decision of that committee before dealing with the subject in the assembly. Is there discussion on the appeal? The president recognizes the member who made the appeal."

After the member and other members have spoken on the appeal the president, may make concluding remarks, then continues to a vote.

President: "All those in favor of sustaining the decision of the presiding officer regarding the motion not being in order say 'aye' [pause]. Those against sustaining the decision of the presiding officer say 'no.' The ayes [noes] have it. The decision of the presiding officer has been sustained [overturned]."

If the decision of the presiding officer is overturned, the presiding officer states the motion that has now been ruled in order.

Table 9.5 gives precedence for a motion to appeal a decision of the presiding officer.

Other Considerations

An opinion of the presiding officer may not be appealed. From time to time a presiding officer may provide an opinion on a subject during discussion. For example, the presiding officer may remark "In my opinion, we

Table 9.5 Precedence Table (Appeal a Decision of the Presiding Officer)

Takes Precedence Over:	Yields To:
All motions pending when the presiding officer rules on a point of order The motion to appeal may not be made unless the presiding officer has ruled on a point.	The motion to postpone temporarily and all privileged motions, provided these motions are of a higher precedence than the last ranked motion pending. It also yields to incidental motions, provided they are truly incidental to the meeting situation at that time. In addition, the motions to limit, extend, and close debate may be applied to the appeal, if the appeal is debatable.

should not permit the member to take the proposed trip." This is a casual remark, not a ruling, and may not be appealed.

A ruling of the presiding officer for which clearly no other interpretation is possible may not be appealed. For example, if the presiding officer rules that a motion to postpone indefinitely is out of order because the pending motion is a motion to amend, which has a higher order of precedence than the motion to postpone indefinitely, this is simply a fact and may not be appealed.

A point of order made when an appeal is pending is ruled upon by the presiding officer and may not be appealed.

Suspend the Rules

The purpose of the motion to *suspend the rules* is to permit a time-limited deviation from a rule of procedure that is interfering with an action the assembly wishes to take.

From time to time situations arise such that dispensing with a procedural rule would permit a meeting to proceed more efficiently. It may be as simple as deviating from the normal order of business, or a parliamentary situation may become so complex or confusing that a procedural shortcut may clear matters up.

When stating the motion, the member need not specify the rule to be suspended but must state the specific activity to be allowed under the suspension. If no time is specified, which is the usual circumstance, the suspension applies only once and to the specific parliamentary situation at hand. However, a suspension is allowable over a series of motions or for the whole meeting. When a suspension of a rule is required over a time period, the motion must be made as a main motion when no other business is pending. See table 9.6.

Not all rules may be suspended. Rules in bylaws, constitutions, and articles of incorporation cannot be suspended unless the rule contains a clause that permits its suspension. In addition, there are certain fundamental rules in parliamentary law that may not be suspended (see chapter 2, "Fundamental Rules of Order"). In summary these are:

- Rules relating to any vote-counting protocol (chapter 10)

- Rules relating to time-dependent activities, such as providing notice

Table 9.6. Suspend the Rules

Characteristic	Required	Further Explanation
Second	Yes	
Debatable	No	Not normally debatable, but restricted debate is allowed when the motion is made as a main motion when no other business is pending.
Amendable	No	There is nothing to amend in *suspend the rules.*
Vote Required	2/3	Suspending a rule is in essence putting in place a new rule of order, even though temporarily, therefore it requires a two-thirds vote.
May Interrupt	No	
May Be Renewed	Yes	The motion to *suspend the rules* may be renewed after progress has been made in debate.
May Be Reconsidered	No	If the motion to *suspend the rules* is disallowed it may not be reconsidered but may be renewed. If the motion to suspend is adopted, it is not useful to reconsider the motion.

- Rules related to quorum requirements
- Rules related to protecting a minority

For example, a vote-counting protocol that requires a 60 percent vote for adoption of a motion may not be suspended; a notice period requiring fourteen days' notice for a nomination for office may not be suspended; a meeting requiring that a majority of the members be present to conduct business may not be suspended; a ballot vote may not be suspended in favor of a voice vote; members' inherent rights in meetings, such as attendance, voting, debating, and running for office, may not be suspended unless restrictions on these rights are contained in the documents of authority or in disciplinary procedures.

The physical method of voting may be suspended, provided the vote-counting protocol is not changed. For example, a motion that requires a majority to adopt and is normally taken by voice vote may be changed to the "serpentine" method of voting (chapter 10) or any other physical method of voting, provided the majority required to adopt remains unchanged.

Let us consider an example:

Member: "Madam President, I move to suspend the rules and permit the amendment to the main motion to be reconsidered."

President: "Under the association's rules an amendment to a main motion may not be reconsidered. The member wishes to suspend the rule to reconsider the amendment. The motion before you is suspend the rules and permit a reconsideration of the amendment. There is no discussion on this motion. All those in favor of suspending the rules say 'aye' [pause]. "All those against suspending the rules say 'no.' The rules are [are not] suspended, and the member may [may not] move a reconsideration of the amendment."

The precedence of a motion to suspend the rules is indicated in table 9.7.

Request to be Excused from a Duty

A motion to *request to be excused from a duty* permits a members to excuse themselves from duties contained in the documents of authority. This is analogous to suspending a substantive rule (not a procedural rule) in the documents of authority. It permits a member, under special circumstances, to communicate those special circumstances to the assembly and to seek relief from the duty.

For example, an officer may be required through the documents of authority to be ex officio a member of an affiliate board. The officer

Table 9.7. Precedence Table (Suspend the Rules)

Takes Precedence Over:	Yields To:
Any motion that is pending when a situation arises that requires a rule to be suspended in order to proceed more effectively or efficiently.	The motion to postpone temporarily and all privileged motions, provided these motions are of a higher precedence than the last ranked motion pending. It also yields to incidental motions, provided they are truly incidental to the meeting situation at that time.

may not be able to fulfill that duty, for various reasons, and may seek to be excused. If the officer is excused, the organization can follow other options in fulfilling its obligations to the affiliate board. This incidental motion may only be made as a main motion. See table 9.8.

Procedure and Example

Member: "Mr. President, I have been transferred from Boston to Los Angeles by my employer for a period of three months. I will be unable to fulfill my duties as secretary of the association during that time. I request to be excused from my duties as secretary for the next three months" (another member may second the motion).

President: "Mr. Secretary will be unable to attend the next three meetings of the association and requests to be excused from his duties as secretary. The motion is (assuming a second), 'Shall Mr. Secretary be excused from his duties as secretary for the next three months?'"

Discussion is permitted, and amendments to the motion are allowed. If the time period had been extensive or the transfer had been permanent, the motion could have been stated as a resignation from

Table 9.8.   Request to be Excused from a Duty

Characteristic	Required	Further Explanation
Second	Yes	The motion is a request from an individual member stated as a main motion. A second is normally assumed.
Debatable	Yes	Fully debatable and may go into the merits of the question.
Amendable	Yes	May be amendable as to the length of time the member is excused from the duty or any other condition under which the member is excused.
Vote Required	Majority	
May Interrupt	No	
May Be Renewed	No	As the request is made as a main motion, it may not be renewed but may be reconsidered.
May Be Reconsidered	Yes	Although the request is an incidental motion, it is stated as a main motion and has the same characters as a main motion. It therefore can be reconsidered.

the position of secretary. It would have been procedurally dealt with in the same manner. Such a motion could be stated as, "Shall the member be excused from all duties of secretary through resignation?"

Although it is common practice in voluntary associations not to accept resignations formally, it is good practice to do so. It allows the association to invoke any bylaw provision to replace the officer, and it sets in motion the process to replace the officer. In addition, it permits the member resigning to end formally all obligations to the association.

The precedence of a request to be excused from a duty, when stated as a motion, is given in table 9.9.

Other Considerations

The request to be excused from a duty is a special construct in parliamentary law that allows an assembly to bypass the rule that bylaws are not suspendable unless the bylaw article contains a clause allowing for its own suspension. In essence, the request suspends an obligation (not a rule of order) in the bylaws. If the obligation is contained in any other document of authority, the request, if allowed, suspends that obligation as well.

Incidental Motions Relating to Information— Request Information

The purpose of the motion to *request information* is to permit a member to ask a question. If any business is pending, the question must be re-

Table 9.9. Precedence Table (Request to be Excused from a Duty When Stated as a Motion)

Takes Precedence Over:	Yields To:
No other motion. May only be made when no other motion is pending.	All subsidary and privileged motions; also incidental motions, provided they are truly incidental to the meeting situation at that time.

lated to that business or to the parliamentary situation. If the question is directed to another member, the presiding officer need only direct the question to that other member for an answer; the president, however, may answer the question if he or she knows the answer. If the question is not directed to a member, the presiding officer may answer it or direct it to another member.

It is improper to seek the floor to ask a question and then advocate a position through debate. In this case any member may raise a point of order, or the presiding officer may do so by calling the member to order.

The question may be related to the parliamentary situation (parliamentary inquiry), if the member is seeking to understand what the parliamentary situation is or desires clarification on previous remarks made. See table 9.10.

To suggest some examples illustrating the procedure:

1. *Member:* "Madam President, I request information. Would the member who last spoke please clarify what she meant when she used the acronym CMS, which was used a number of times!"

Table 9.10. Request Information

Characteristic	Required	Further Explanation
Second	No	The motion is a request from an individual for information.
Debatable	No	There is nothing to debate.
Amendable	No	Not technically amendable, but the member may ask supplementary questions if the answer is unclear.
Vote Required	No	It is a request and is handled by the presiding officer or passed to another to answer.
May Interrupt	No	A member may not interrupt another speaker to ask a question.
May Be Renewed	Yes	The same question may be asked again if future discussion indicates that an incorrect or misleading or unclear answer was previously given.
May Be Reconsidered	No	

President: "My understanding is that CMS means 'cycloconverter media system.' However, I do not know what 'cycloconverter' means. Can the member clarify the terminology?"

2. *Member:* "Mr. President, I am unsure how to vote on this motion. Could the president explain the impact on the association if the motion is defeated or if the motion is adopted?"
3. *Member:* "Mr. President, I am unsure which motion is pending. Can the president explain the parliamentary situation?"
4. *Member:* "Mr. President, would it be in order now to postpone the motion until the March meeting?"

See table 9.11 for the precedence of a request for information.

Incidental Motions Relating to Efficient Meetings

Consider By Paragraph

The purpose of the motion to *consider by paragraph* is to permit the assembly to consider each section of a proposal in succession rather than open the complete proposal to debate and amendment. This permits a more orderly progression. The presiding officer may suggest this method of proceeding, or a member who believes it appropriate may do so. See table 9.12.

If consideration by paragraph is ordered, the presiding officer opens the first section of the proposal to debate and amendment. When that is complete, the presiding officer moves to the next section; the process is repeated until the complete proposal has been debated and amended.

Table 9.11. Precedence Table (Request Information)

Takes Precedence Over:	Yields To:
All motions	The motion to postpone temporarily and all privileged motions, provided these motions are of a higher precedence than the last ranked motion pending. It also yields to incidental motions, provided they are truly incidental to the meeting situation at that time.

Table 9.12. Consider by Paragraph

Characteristic	Required	Further Explanation
Second	Yes	
Debatable	Yes	Restricted debate is allowed as to the different manners of considering a motion by paragraph.
Amendable	Yes	If the proposal could be considered in a different manner, an amendment may be proposed to do so.
Vote Required	Majority	
May Interrupt	No	
May Be Renewed	Yes	If the motion has been defeated, it may be renewed after some business has transpired.
May Be Reconsidered	No	If the motion is defeated, it may be renewed (see above). If the motion has been adopted a member may move after some business has transpired to consider the resolution as a whole (same rules as consider by paragraph).

The presiding officer then opens up the complete proposal to amendment and debate. When the complete proposal has been debated and further amended, the proposal is voted on as a whole.

At any time during the process of considering a proposal by paragraph, any member may move that the proposal be "considered as a whole." If seconded and then adopted, this cuts short the consideration by paragraph and opens up the whole proposal to amendment and debate.

While processing a section, motions to limit, extend, and close debate are permitted but if adopted apply only to the section. All other subsidiary motions (except postpone indefinitely) and all privileged motions are applicable but apply to the whole proposal. Applicable incidental motions are also permitted.

To give an example illustrating the procedure:

Member: "Mr. President, I move that we consider the bylaws revision article by article" (second).

President: "It is moved and seconded that the bylaws be considered article by article. This means that we will open each article to debate and to amendment. When we are complete, the full bylaws will be

Table 9.13. Precedence Table (Consider by Paragraph)

Takes Precedence Over:	Yields To:
Main motions. It may only be moved when a main motion is pending.	To all subsidary and privileged motions. It also yields to other incidental motions, provided they are truly incidental to the meeting situation at that time.

open to debate and amendment." The president then proceeds to vote on the motion to consider the bylaws article by article.

The precedence of a motion to consider by paragraph is given in table 9.13.

Request to Withdraw a Motion

The purpose of the motion to *request to withdraw a motion* is to permit a member who proposed a motion to withdraw it prior to the vote being taken. The member may believe that the motion will be handily defeated or decide after hearing the discussion that the motion is not in the best interest of the organization or that to proceed to the vote would be an inefficient use of the members' time. See table 9.14.

The request to withdraw is normally granted through general consent, but if an objection is made, a motion may be proposed by

Table 9.14. Request to Withdraw a Motion

Characteristic	Required	Further Explanation
Second	Yes	Normally handled by general consent, but if made as a motion it requires a second. A second is implied if a member, other than the requester, proposes a motion.
Debatable	No	There is nothing to debate.
Amendable	No	There is nothing to amend.
Vote Required	Majority	If proposed as a motion it requires a majority vote to adopt.
May Interrupt	No	
May Be Renewed	Yes	May be renewed after progress has been made in debate.
May Be Reconsidered	No	If defeated the motion may be renewed (see above). If adopted, the motion that was withdrawn may be made again during the meeting.

the requester or any other member, or assumed by the presiding officer.

Any motion may be withdrawn with the permission of the assembly. A main motion may be withdrawn even when subsidiary or other motions are pending and are attached to the main motion. If a main motion is withdrawn in these circumstances, all attached motions are also withdrawn.

When a motion is first proposed and seconded, but before the presiding officer states it, it belongs to the proposer of the motion. It may be withdrawn or modified without the permission of the assembly. Once the presiding officer has stated a motion, it belongs to the assembly, and permission is required to withdraw it.

If a motion is withdrawn after being stated by the presiding officer, it is recorded in the minutes, provided it would have been recorded in the minutes if not withdrawn. If a motion is withdrawn it may be renewed later in the meeting.

To give two examples:

1. Assume Member A has made a motion. An amendment and a motion to postpone are also pending.
   Member A: "Mr. President, I request that the main motion be withdrawn."
   President: "Member A has requested that the main motion be withdrawn. Is there any objection to the request being granted? [pause]. There being no objection, the motion is withdrawn."
   The amendment and the motion to postpone fall to the ground.
2. Assume Member A has appealed a decision of the presiding officer and that some discussion has taken place.
   Member A: "Mr. President, I request that the appeal be withdrawn."
   President: "Member A has requested that the appeal be withdrawn. Is there any objection to the appeal being withdrawn?"
   Member B: "I object."
   Member C (after recognition): "Mr. President, I move that the request to withdraw the appeal be granted" (implied second by member A).
   The president would now state the request to withdraw as a motion and take the vote.

Table 9.15. Precedence Table (Request to Withdraw a Motion)

Takes Precedence Over:	Yields To:
All motions	The motion to postpone temporarily and all privileged motions, provided these motions are of a higher precedence than the last ranked motion pending. It also yields to incidental motions, provided they are truly incidental to the meeting situation at that time.

See table 9.15 for the precedence of a request to withdraw a motion.

Incidental Motions Relating to Voting and Nominations

Division of a Question

The purpose of the motion *division of a question* is to permit the assembly to debate and vote separately on independent motions (or resolutions) that have been proposed as a single motion (or resolution). Division of a question applies only to main motions or resolutions. See table 9.16.

Table 9.16. Division of a Question

Characteristic	Required	Further Explanation
Second	No	If the individual motions are truly independent the question must be divided on the demand of one member.
Debatable	No	There is nothing to debate.
Amendable	No	There is nothing to amend.
Vote Required	No	If proposed as a motion it requires a majority vote to adopt.
May Interrupt	No	
May Be Renewed	No	If denied or permitted by the presiding officer the ruling may be appealed.
May Be Reconsidered	No	If denied or permitted by the presiding officer the ruling may be appealed.

If a member believes that the motion as proposed comprises independent motions and that it may not be possible to vote properly on the composite motion, the member may propose a division to permit a "yes" vote on one part and a "no" vote on the other. This is analogous to the concept of a consent agenda, where a member may demand that an individual item on the consent agenda be removed from the agenda for individual consideration.

The test of whether a composite motion may be divided is if any individual motion were to be adopted and all other individual motions defeated, the motion adopted could be acted on. For example, a motion "to purchase a typewriter and to give it to the executive secretary" is not divisible into "Purchase a typewriter" and "Give it to the executive secretary"; if the motion to purchase a typewriter were defeated, the second part, even if adopted, could not be acted on. If a member wishes to purchase a typewriter but not give it to the executive secretary, the proper procedure is to move to amend the motion by striking out "and to give it to the executive secretary."

When a motion to divide the question is first made, the proposer must delineate clearly the division proposed. The proposer may also suggest that a single motion be removed from the composite motion to be debated and voted on separately. The presiding officer, in the first instance, will decide if the composite motion is divisible but may if unsure, seek guidance from the assembly. The presiding officer makes the decision on the division, which is subject to appeal.

A series of two or more motions may be divided at any time prior to the vote, even if close debate has been ordered.

To give two examples showing the procedure:

1. Assume the following message is pending:
   Resolved, That the association lease the second floor of our headquarters to PSM Ltd.,
   Resolved, That the association refurbish the first floor of the headquarters building,
   Resolved, That the association bid to host the national convention in 2004, and
   Resolved, That the association open negotiations with the city to provide sport services to the city.

Member: "Mr. President, I request that we divide the resolution into its four component parts and debate and vote on each separately."

President: "The resolution is divisible, and we will deal with each separately. The motion before you is, 'That the association lease the second floor of our headquarters to PSM Ltd.' Is there any discussion?"

The president takes each of the other three component parts of the resolution and presents them as individual motions to be debated and voted on separately.

2. Using the same example above, a member wishing to vote for three of the four resolve clauses but against the motion regarding hosting the national convention would say, "Mr. President, I wish to take from the resolution the resolve clause dealing with the national convention and deal with it separately." The president would allow the demand and say, "The resolve clause 'That the association bid to host the national convention in 2004' will be dealt with as a separate motion."

The precedence of a division of a question is indicated in table 9.17.

Doubt the Vote

The purpose of a motion to *doubt the vote* is to permit a member to demand that the vote be taken again. If a member believes that a voice vote was too close to call, that a vote result announced by the presiding officer is wrong, or that the assembly is confused regarding the taking of the vote, the member may demand that the vote be taken again or, at the discretion of the presiding officer, be taken by a different

Table 9.17.   Precedence Table (Division of a Question)

Takes Precedence Over:	Yields To:
Main motions that may be divided	All motions except another main motion. Subsidary motions made while *division of the question* is pending are applied to the main motion.

method. At the discretion of the presiding officer, the vote may be taken in the same manner, by a rising vote, or if the assembly is small enough, by a counted vote. The demand to take the vote again may be made only after the vote is taken and before the presiding officer states the next motion. See table 9.18.

If a member renews the motion to doubt the vote and if the presiding officer believes the member is being dilatory, the presiding officer should disallow the motion, subject to appeal. If the presiding officer is uncertain, the vote should be taken by a different method, including a count if necessary.

Procedure and Example

Assume a vote has been taken by voice.

Member (without waiting to be recognized and before the president has announced the vote result): "Mr President, I doubt the vote."

President: "The vote has been doubted. The vote will be taken again. Those in favor, please rise [pause]. Those against, please rise [pause]. The noes [or ayes] have it, and the motion is defeated [adopted]."

The member could have waited until the president announced the vote then called out "I doubt the vote."

Table 9.18. Doubt the Vote

Characteristic	Required	Further Explanation
Second	No	It is a demand from an individual member.
Debatable	No	There is nothing to debate.
Amendable	No	There is nothing to amend.
Vote Required	No	It is a demand, and no vote is required.
May Interrupt	Yes	High priority is given to ensuring that the vote count is correct, therfore a member who doubts the vote may interrupt a speaker or the presiding officer
May Be Renewed	Yes	If the vote is taken in the same manner as before or if the rising vote is inconclusive, the member may again doubt the vote.
May Be Reconsidered	No	

Table 9.19. Precedence Table (Doubt the Vote)

Takes Precedence Over:	Yields To:
All motions that have just been voted on	No other motion. Once a vote has begun, no other business may interfere

If the president takes the second vote and is still unsure of the vote result, she may take a count if the assembly is small, or in a large assembly, order the tellers to take a count.

The precedence of a motion to doubt the vote is as given in table 9.19.

Other Considerations

If the presiding officer is unwilling to take a count, any member may make a motion to take a count: "Madam President, I move that the vote be counted." This requires a second and a majority vote. If adopted, the presiding officer must take a counted vote. The presiding officer should be liberal in granting, by general consent, counted votes. If the motion to take a count is abused, the presiding officer may rule the motion out of order, subject to appeal.

Request a Physical Method of Voting

The purpose of the motion to *request a physical method of voting* (chapter 10) is to permit a member to propose a different method of casting the vote from the usual voice vote or show of hands. In making the motion a member attempts to ensure that the vote count is accurate and correct. The proposal for a physical vote may specify a single motion or a series of motions to which the physical vote applies. See table 9.20.

The most common proposal is that a vote be taken by ballot. Other physical voting methods, such as the serpentine vote, roll call, and a counted show of hands, may be proposed. The method proposed, which should increase the accuracy of the count, is normally handled by general consent. If a member objects to the method of voting or proposes a different method, a majority vote decides.

If a physical method of voting is contained in the bylaws, it may not be varied through this motion unless the bylaws allow for their own suspension. For example, a ballot vote for an election may not be changed to a voice vote or a serpentine vote if a ballot vote is required in the bylaws. Also, a vote counting protocol (chapter 10) may not be amended through this motion.

Table 9.20. Request a Physical Method of Voting

Characteristic	Required	Further Explanation
Second	Yes	Requires a second but is normally handled by general consent.
Debatable	No	There is nothing to debate.
Amendable	Yes	May be amended as to a different method of voting or amended as to the motions to which the method of voting will apply.
Vote Required	Majority	If not handled by general consent, it requires a majority vote.
May Interrupt	No	
May Be Renewed	Yes	It may be renewed if the vote count is inconclusive on the underlying motion.
May Be Reconsidered	No	It may be renewed (see above).

Let us take an example:

Member: "Mr. President, I request that when we take the vote on the two bylaw amendments, the vote be taken by serpentine vote" (chapter 10).

President: "The member has requested that when we take the vote on the bylaw amendment, we take it by serpentine vote. Is there any objection to taking the vote on the bylaws by serpentine vote? [pause]. There being no objection, when we take the vote on the bylaw amendments it will be by serpentine vote."

Table 9.21 indicates the precedence of a motion to request a physical method of voting.

Table 9.21 Precedence Table (Request a Physical Method of Voting)

Takes Precedence Over:	Yields To:
Any motion or series of motions to be voted on	The motion to postpone temporarily and all privileged motions, provided these motions are of a higher precedence than the last ranked motion pending. It also yields to other incidental motions, provided they are truly incidental to the meeting situation at that time.

CHAPTER TEN

~

Voting Methods

Definition and Terms

- Voting—The process, physical and procedural, of turning individual preferences into a group decision.
- Legal Vote—A vote cast by one who is authorized to vote. A legal vote[1] is counted, recorded, reported, and used in calculating the vote required to adopt or elect.
- Illegal Vote—A vote cast by one who is not authorized to vote. An illegal vote is recorded, and reported but is not used in calculating the vote required to adopt or elect.
- Spoiled Ballot —A legal vote that has some irregularity, such that the tellers cannot allocate the vote to a candidate or a proposal (such as a ballot marked for more than the number of candidates required).
- Blank Ballot—A vote cast that has no identifiable marks. This type of ballot is discarded and not counted as a vote.
- Majority—A number greater than half of a total. In voting, the "total" is usually of "those voting." Therefore a majority vote (when unqualified) means more than half of those voting.

---

[1] Throughout this text a "legal vote cast" is simply referred to as a "vote cast."

- Plurality Vote—Where there are more than two propositions or more than two candidates, the proposition or candidate with the most votes is declared the winner.
- Two-Thirds Vote—A vote that requires at least two-thirds of the votes cast to adopt a proposition.
- Double-Majority Vote—A requirement that majorities on two levels of an organization vote for a proposal before it is adopted.
- Vote-Counting Protocol—The procedure by which individual votes are transformed into a group decision.
- Minimum Complement Required to Adopt or Elect—A requirement that some minimum number of votes be cast in favor to adopt a proposal or elect a candidate.
- Majority of the Quorum—A number greater than half of a defined quorum. If a quorum is defined as ten members present, a majority of the quorum is six.

Democracy and Majority Rule

One of the principles of democracy is that everyone has a right to an opinion and to take action on that opinion. However, when opinions diverge, which is often the case, there must be a way for a group of people with a common goal to come together, make a collective decision, and take action on that decision. A group decision on an issue can be made when there is sufficient information available to focus the group on a few possible responses to the issue; that is, information (another important right in a democracy) helps focus the group and helps narrow its choices. However, more than information is required to bring a group to a unified decision.

Another principle of democracy is that a group needs to agree ahead of time on how it might make a group decision, as well as a commitment on everyone's part to accept that decision. By this agreement—a social contract—the group decides between choices by selecting the option that has the largest following—that is, the choice with which more than half of the group agrees. In other words it decides by voting and using the rule of the majority. Just as important as majority rule, however, is agreement that all will accept and support the result and move on to the next group decision. To that end, the minority must be afforded by pre-agreement the right to attack the ideas and opinions of the majority and yet expect to be protected from reprisal (yet another important principle of a democracy). By joining a group that operates using democratic principles, members implicitly agree that the majority will rule, that collective decisions will be accepted, that the minority will have an opportunity to disagree, and that the minority will be protected.

Are there other ways to make a group decision? One could pick one of the members of the group randomly, give that person the title of "autocrat," and let the "autocrat" make all the decisions. The group could get lucky and find a wise "autocrat" who has the welfare of the other members at heart. This is the very best one could hope for, but even that would not satisfy most members. They would quickly tire even of a wise autocrat, because human nature demands freedom of action; an individual making all decisions is the antithesis of this freedom. When autocracy is replaced by the concept of majority rule the individual freedom returns, which for most individuals is a much more satisfying arrangement. Another option is force—to have those with the power to use force make the decisions. Force strips all freedom from the individual; it not only inhibits the individual from freedom of action but often restricts the individual from even having opinions. Force is not a desirable option in decision making.

But there is more to majority rule than freedom of action. Majority rule means that a group of people throw all their ideas together, select their best parts, and agree on the sum of the parts. There is a solidifying of opinion, and finally a decision is made. That is, when more than half can support the decision, the decision is considered made by the full group, not just the majority—as the minority have previously agreed to go along with the majority. The minority has had its say and a safe opportunity to sway the majority, the majority has made the decision, and the group moves ahead.

Methods of Voting

When voting is discussed most people think of picking up a ballot, marking it, placing it in a ballot box, and then awaiting the result of the vote. This is the physical aspect of voting. There is, however, a largely unknown procedure that occurs between placing the ballot in the box and the announcement of the result. This is the procedure of turning the individual votes cast into a result—the *vote-counting protocol*.

The American presidency is decided by a very unusual vote-counting protocol called the Electoral College. The votes cast by the populace are counted, and the results (decided by a plurality vote) in each state are used by the state governments to elect slates of electors. Each state's electors in turn vote for the president and transmit a list of all persons voted for in the state to the president of the Senate. On a specified date the president *pro tempore* of the Senate opens and counts the votes from each state. The constitution reads, "The Person having the greatest Number of Votes shall be the President, if such Number be a majority of the Whole Number of Electors appointed."[2] This is a very complex vote-counting protocol written into the Constitution by the framers in 1787. It is actually much more complex than briefly described above, as there are differences in choosing electors among the various states; in some cases electors are mandated to cast their votes for a candidate, while others are free to vote for whomever they please. The overall vote-counting protocol is intended to protect the smaller states from being dominated by the larger, vote-rich states. Three times in the history of the United States the Electoral College process has produced a result different from the popular vote. This shows the importance of the vote-counting protocol.

The physical aspects of voting in the United States elections also vary among the states. In the election of November 2000 this became painfully obvious. The country watched in amazement as the result of the election for president hung in the balance for many weeks because the ballots used in the state of Florida were found to be defective. The integrity of the election result was compromised because the physical aspects of the count were suspect.

Fortunately, most votes in meetings, which include voting on motions and in elections, are not as complex as those for the presidency of the United States. Electronic devices are not yet commonly used; most votes are taken by voice or a show of hands. In elections, the most com-

---

[2] The Constitution of the United States, Article II, Section 1

mon physical way to vote is by marking a ballot and depositing it in a ballot box. The most common vote-counting protocol, whether the vote is on a motion or in election, is a majority of those voting.

There are, however, many other ways of physically voting and of turning those votes into a result. Each has its place in meetings and elections. The remainder of the chapter describes these various ways of voting.

The Two Parts of Voting

As implied above, every vote has two parts:

- The physical vote
- The vote-counting protocol

The *physical vote* relates to the physical method of casting the vote and the physical method of counting the vote. The *vote counting protocol* relates to the way the individual votes are processed to make a group decision. Both of these aspects of voting are very important. The physical aspects of voting must be meticulously planned. This is particularly true when voting for candidates for office, as the integrity of the election process may otherwise be called into question. The vote-counting protocol must be correctly selected and agreed upon beforehand to ensure that the vote result accurately reflects the wishes of the voters. The vote-counting protocol should be included in the documents of authority; if the documents of authority are silent, the vote-counting protocol is a majority of the votes cast. The vote-counting protocol may not be suspended.

The Physical Vote

In contrast to the vote-counting protocol, the method of taking the physical vote need be included in the documents of authority only if it is a mail vote or electronic vote. It may be included in the documents of authority if the organization wishes certain types of decisions to be made by particular kinds of physical votes. For example, a requirement that ballot votes be taken for elections should be included in the documents of authority. If contained in the bylaws, a requirement to take the vote by ballot or by mail may not be suspended.

The following physical methods of voting are the most common:

- The presiding officer decides, without objection (by consensus)
- A voice vote
- A show of hands
- A standing vote
- A serpentine vote
- A roll-call vote
- A ballot vote
- A mail vote
- An electronic vote

Presiding Officer Decides, without Objection

When the presiding officer senses that a motion has no opposition and is likely to be adopted, the most efficient way to handle it is to say, "If there is no objection, the motion is adopted [pause]. There being no objection, the motion is adopted." The skill and experience of the presiding officer is paramount in disposing of a motion in this way; it should be used on only certain requests, inconsequential motions, friendly or inconsequential amendments, and motions assumed by the presiding officer.

For example, if the motion pending is "That the association purchase the one-acre lot to the south of 101 Scotia Street" and a member makes a motion (seconded) to amend by inserting the words, "known as Shaw's Café" after the word "lot," and it is generally known that the building is in fact known as Shaw's Café, the presiding officer says, "If there is no objection we will add the words 'known as Shaw's Café' after the word 'lot.'" After a short pause, and if there is no objection, the presiding officer continues, "There being no objection, the motion to add the words 'known as Shaw's Café' after the word 'lot' is adopted. The motion now before you is . . ." The presiding officer repeats the motion in full, and debate continues.

If there was an objection—and it only takes one member to object—the presiding officer says, "There is an objection. The motion before you is to amend the main motion to add the words 'known as Shaw's Café' after the word 'lot.' Is there any discussion on the amendment?"

In another example, the presiding officer, recognizing that it may be time for a break, may assume a motion by saying, "It appears that the meeting needs a break. If there is no objection the meeting will take a fifteen minute recess [pause]. There being no objection, the meeting stands in recess for fifteen minutes." If there were an objection the presiding officer would continue with the meeting or take a vote on the question to recess.

A member may make a request to introduce an important person (a nonmember) to the meeting. Again the presiding officer, understanding the sense of the meeting, may permit the introduction of the person without objection.

The presiding officer has to be careful that liberal use of the words "If there is no objection" not be seen as railroading the assembly. Properly employed, it is a powerful technique for keeping the meeting moving, and most members will appreciate the skill of the presiding officer in ensuring the efficient use of everyone's time.

Voice Vote

A voice vote is used when the vote-counting protocol is a majority of the votes cast. The presiding officer determines the majority of the votes cast by volume of sound. A voice vote may not be used when a two-thirds vote is required or if the majority is not of the votes cast but a qualified majority, such as a majority of those present. The presiding officer calls for the vote by announcing, "All those in favor say 'aye' [pause]; all those against say 'no.'" On hearing the vote, the presiding officer says, "In my opinion the ayes [or noes] have it," pauses, and then continues, "The ayes [or noes] have it, and the motion is adopted [or lost]."

If the presiding officer feels that a representative number of members have not voted or are unsure of the motion or are confused, the presiding officer has a duty to restate the motion and call for the vote again.

If the presiding officer is unsure of the result of the voice vote, a show of hands or a standing vote is taken; if the result is still not plain, a count of the vote is taken. The presiding officer, as guardian of the assembly, has discretion in calling for a counted vote to ensure accuracy of the result.

As described previously, a member may call for a standing vote by calling out, "I doubt the vote," immediately upon the voice vote being taken or immediately after the presiding officer has announced the result. This signifies that the member believes that the vote is too close for the presiding officer to call or that the presiding officer may be mistaken in his or her determination of the vote. This action by a member is a demand for a standing vote (or show of hands), and the presiding officer must comply. If the standing vote is indecisive, the presiding officer counts the votes, or orders the tellers to count them, while the members are standing. A serpentine vote (see below) may also be used to count the votes.

A member, unlike the presiding officer, may not demand a count but may request one. This may be granted by general consent or by a vote. The presiding officer should be liberal in granting such requests unless a pattern of abuse is evident or the request is clearly dilatory. In any case, a voice vote on the matter of a counted vote is final when announced.

Show of Hands and Standing Vote

A vote by a show of hands and a standing vote are equivalent methods. At the discretion of the presiding officer a vote may be taken by a show of hands in preference to a standing vote. In small assemblies a show of hands would be as accurate as a standing vote and would be more efficient. In large assemblies the standing vote is likely to be more accurate.

A show of hands or standing vote is used when a two-thirds vote is required or when demanded by a member on an indecisive vote. If the result remains inconclusive, the presiding officer may order a count to be taken.

Serpentine Vote

A serpentine vote is an alternative method of conducting a count in which individuals in the assembly count their own votes. The presiding officer asks those members in favor of the motion to stand. After standing, the first member starts counting ("One!") and sits down; the second member continues the count ("Two!") and sits down. The process "snakes" around the assembly until all the votes are counted and all the aye voters are seated. The aye vote is recorded. The presiding officer then asks all those against the motion to stand and follow an identical procedure. The presiding officer then announces the vote count and the result.

The serpentine vote is an efficient and accurate way of counting the vote. It may be used at the discretion of the presiding officer or ordered by majority vote of the assembly.

Roll-Call Vote

A roll-call vote is considered the most accurate method of voting. A motion to use a roll-call vote requires a majority to adopt unless a lesser number is stated in the documents of authority. In many quasi-governmental agencies and in local governmental bodies the documents of authority mandate a roll-call vote for certain types of motions.

When a roll-call vote is mandated by the documents of authority or ordered by the assembly, the secretary calls out each voting member by name; each member answers, "Aye," "No," or "Abstain." This continues until all members have been polled. The secretary tallies the vote and hands it to the presiding officer. The presiding officer assures himself of the accuracy of the tally before announcing the vote count and the result.

The vote of each member is recorded in the minutes, as is the vote tally and the vote result announced by the presiding officer.

Ballot Vote

A ballot vote is a secret vote. It is normally used in elections but may be used on any motion when ordered by a majority vote of the assembly. The ballot vote allows members to cast their vote privately, which in turn allows members to vote their true preferences, if they might otherwise for some reason feel constrained from doing so.

When it is known that a proposition will be voted on by ballot the ballot paper should be made out in advance, with the question shown, as on figure 10.1.

In the event that the members order a ballot vote on a motion, the staff should have on hand a number of blank ballots of different colors, with each color having a unique three-character alphanumeric code, as shown at figure 10.2. The color and the alphanumeric code serve to protect doubly the integrity of the vote.

Figure 10.1.   Sample Ballot, for Planned Ballot Vote

<u>Ballot</u>
(mark with a check or an X)
Shall the association purchase the AGS System?

Yes _____
No _____

These ballots are to be well protected and handed out just prior to the vote by the tellers committee. If the matter is important enough, the credentials committee may hand out the ballots after checking each member against the membership list.

This parliamentary authority advocates sparing use of the ballot vote, if it must be used at all. In a democratic organization, where people stand on issues should be known; the ballot vote should not be used to hide one's vote. The counterargument is that social pressures influence how a person might vote, and the ballot vote allows one to vote one's own conscience. Some quasi-government agencies and local government disallow ballot votes, except for elections.

Mail Vote

A mail vote is a useful voting method when it is inconvenient or costly for a group to meet in assembly. It may also be used for emergency action that requires the authorization of the group. It may also be used by small bodies, such as committees, to take a formal vote on a motion that has been discussed by mail. A mail vote must be authorized in the bylaws. The details of the procedure used to take the mail vote should be defined in a lower-ranking document of authority than the bylaws.

Figure 10.2.   Sample Ballot, for Ballot Vote Ordered by the Assembly

---

<u>Ballot</u>
(mark with a check or an X)
Question D4R*

Yes _____
No _____

---

*Three-character alphanumeric code protects the vote

If the documents of authority are silent on the minimum number of votes required to be cast for a valid vote, the number received by mail is the minimum number of votes required. One has to be careful, however, that only one or two votes sent by mail may decide the vote. As in a ballot vote, blank ballots are discarded and not counted.

A mail vote may be secret or open. When a nonsecret vote on a motion is required to be taken by mail, the information sent to each member includes the following:

- A voting slip (ballot) with a clear statement of the motion, a place to vote, and a place to record the voter's name and signature

- Any relevant information pro or con the motion

Administratively, the following is required:

1. A specially marked, self-addressed envelope to be used for returning the vote.
2. The deadline for casting the vote (using postmark).
3. The address to which the vote has to be sent.
4. Instructions on how to mark the voting slip, including name and signature.
5. The date on which the votes will be tallied and the date the result will be announced.

When each specially marked envelope is received at the place to which the votes are to be sent (usually to the head office), it is held until the date the tellers committee is to take possession of them (after the deadline date). In no circumstances should the votes be counted until the deadline date has passed. The tellers open each envelope and check the member's name, and if necessary the signature, against the organization's official membership list. The vote is also recorded. All voting slips are put in safekeeping. Late votes and the envelope in which they were sent are put in safekeeping; they do not affect the result.

When the vote on a motion is to be secret, the only difference is that a double-envelope process is used. A second, smaller envelope is furnished in which to place the ballot. In addition, the member's name and signature are not on the ballot but on the inner envelope. The tellers use the inner envelope and not the ballot to identify the member as a legal voter.

When the vote is for an election (usually a secret vote), the process is the same except that the information provided to the voter does not refer to a motion but to the candidates. Each candidate must be afforded the same opportunity to provide information to the electorate.

One practical method of ensuring that an election by mail produces a result is *preferential voting*. This method, with an example, is described in chapter 11, "Nominations and Elections." Plurality voting is not recommended for mail elections, as it does not guarantee a result; two candidates may have equal numbers of votes. Preferential voting can be designed to guarantee, for all practical purposes, a result.

This parliamentary authority does not advocate mixing voting by mail with voting at meetings on the same motion or election. If the organization does use such a method, it must clearly define how elections are to be decided in the event of "no election"—that is, if no candidate receives the required number of votes to elect. Such an outcome may cause untold delay in the election and substantial cost.

Electronic Vote

There are a number of ways to vote electronically. The most common are:

- Telephone

- Internet

- Computer (using a keypad)

Behind all of these methods of voting electronically are computer and communication devices. The telephone and the Internet allow members to vote at a distance; the computer keypad is more commonly used while the members are in assembly.

These methods have a number of common characteristics. They all require some instruction, because some voters may not be familiar with the equipment; the processes or devices not only accept the vote but

tally the vote and produce a final result; the processes also require so-
phisticated security precautions to ensure that nonvoters do not vote,
that voters do not vote twice, and that once cast the votes remain pri-
vate and confidential, if privacy is required.

Many organizations are now beginning to use electronic voting at
meetings, using keypads. It provides for more accurate counting and
displays results in seconds. This type of voting is particularly useful in
large assemblies and especially when a double-majority vote is used. It
may also be used to verify a quorum and conduct elections. Vote-
counting protocols such as preferential voting, the Borda count, and
approval voting (see below) become much more efficient in elections
when votes are counted electronically. Many companies provide systems that allow members to vote electronically. The cost of such means
of voting is now within the reach of many associations.

In votes at meetings using electronic means, even if the computer
equipment has the capability to produce the result, the result does not
become official until announced by the presiding officer. This allows
the presiding officer, and others, to check that the result is at least reasonable (that votes cast are not greater than the members present, for
example) before announcing it.

The Vote-Counting Protocol
In meetings, most decisions are made between adopting a proposition and
not adopting it—voting for a motion or against it. In elections, the decision is often between two candidates only. In both of these cases a
decision is normally made by a majority of the votes cast, but not always.
Sometimes the organization has decided that a decision is to be made by
a majority of those present (by placing that rule in a document of authority). In other cases a majority of the entire membership is required.

For example, an organization has fifty members, forty of whom are
in attendance at a meeting. Their election vote-counting protocol
calls for a majority of those present to elect the organization's president. There are two candidates. The votes cast are twenty for candidate A, nineteen for candidate B, and one blank ballot. A majority of
those present is twenty-one, so there is no election, and a second vote
is required. If the vote-counting protocol had been a majority of the
votes cast, candidate A would have been elected (votes cast total

thirty-nine, and a majority of thirty-nine is twenty). If the vote-counting protocol had been a majority of the entire membership, twenty-six votes would have been needed to elect a candidate. These examples show that depending upon the vote-counting protocol, elections do not always produce a result (a winner), even with only two candidates running.

The above example, using only two choices, shows the importance of selecting the correct vote-counting protocol. It is even more important when there are more than two choices to be selected from. The vote-counting protocol then becomes crucial, because the results of the vote may be inconsistent with the general will of the assembly. For example, plurality voting in elections in many Western democracies has provided many election results that are recognised as inconsistent with the general will.

Dr. Donald Saari[3] provides the following example.[4] In the 1991 gubernatorial race in Louisiana, David Duke, former governor Edwin Edwards, and the incumbent governor, Buddy Roemer faced off in the election. Duke was a former leader of the Ku Klux Klan and a leader of a neo-Nazi party; Edwards had been indicted for corruption in his previous term and was considered a womanizer; while Roemer had made controversial decisions in his term in office. It was assumed, however, that Roemer would defeat either Duke or Edwards one on one. As it turned out, Roemer finished last in the election. The vote-counting protocol was plurality voting. Roemer was eliminated from the runoff election. This left Edwards to defeat Duke, in what became known as the "Krook versus Klan" election. This is an example where the vote-counting protocol—plurality plus dropping candidates—contributed to what was considered an odd result. Roemer, who would have likely defeated either of the other candidates head to head, did not make the final vote.

The following are the most common vote-counting protocols required to adopt a proposal or to elect a person to office:

- Majority of the votes cast

- Majority of those present and legally entitled to cast a vote

---

[3] Prof. Donald G. Saari, University of California, Irvine
[4] Saari, *Geometry of Voting*, p. 72, Heidelberg, Ger: Springer-Verlag, 1994.

- Majority of the entire membership who are legally entitled to cast a vote

- Plurality of the votes cast

- Two-thirds of the votes cast[5]

- Any other percentage or fraction of the votes cast[5]

- Double majority of the votes cast[5]

- Other protocols

The *majority of votes cast* vote-counting protocol and its variants have been explained through examples earlier in this chapter. Plurality, double-majority, and the two-thirds vote are now analyzed.

Plurality

The plurality protocol allows the person with the most votes to be elected or the proposal with the most votes to be adopted. It is mainly used in elections but is sometimes used when one or two choices are to be selected from a large number of proposals. When there are only two candidates or only two proposals, the plurality protocol and the "majority of votes cast" protocol are identical and will produce the same results.

The plurality protocol can diverge dramatically in its results from the majority protocol, however, when there are as few as three candidates or proposals. An example given earlier in this chapter on the Louisiana gubernatorial race 1991 illustrates how vote-splitting occurs when there are more than two candidates. Two candidates who have similar platforms are very likely to split the vote. This has occurred in Canadian federal elections for a number of years (2000 and 1996 general elections), in which the Reform Party (now the Canadian Alliance Party) and the Progressive Conservative Party, both right-wing parties, fielded candidates in most ridings, split the right-wing vote, and allowed the federal Liberal Party to win handsomely with as little as 38 percent of the popular vote.

---

[5] These protocols, like majority, may be qualified as to those present and to the entire membership

The reason this occurs is that most vote-counting protocols do not account for a voter's second or third choice. This is especially true where the vote-counting protocol is plurality. Information that the voter has (second and third choices) is not communicated in the casting of the vote and hence is not used in determining the result. There are voting protocols—such as preferential voting, approval voting, Condorcet voting, and the Borda count protocol—that do take into account other information and choices that the voter may make and use to get a fairer result. These other vote-counting protocols, since they apply more commonly to elections, are defined in more depth in chapter 11.

Two-Thirds of the Votes Cast

This vote-counting protocol is similar to the "majority of votes cast" protocol, except that the threshold to adopt a proposal is raised from more than half to at least two-thirds of the votes cast. The physical aspects of taking a two-thirds vote are different from those of a majority vote. The two-thirds vote should rarely be taken by voice, as it is difficult to distinguish whether the volume of sound is in fact two-thirds or greater for the ayes than for the noes. The two-thirds vote should be by a show of hands, a standing vote, or some method of counting.

The two-thirds vote is used when the vote infringes on the right of a member. For example, the motion to close debate removes from all members the right to speak—thus it requires a two-thirds vote. The two-thirds vote is often used to amend an organization's bylaws—reflecting a decision of the membership that bylaws should not be readily changed. This voting requirement for bylaw amendments must be contained in the bylaws themselves.

This parliamentary authority advocates minimum use of the two-thirds vote. The two-thirds vote not only protects the minority but allows the minority to frustrate the majority. One of the principles of democracy is that the majority be permitted to rule. The two-thirds vote severely limits the rule of the majority and therefore should be sparingly used.

Any Other Percentage or Fraction of the Votes Cast

The most common fraction of the votes used in meetings is the two-thirds vote. However, an organization may define the vote-counting protocol to be any fraction of the votes cast. For example, some organizations use 60 percent as the fraction of votes required to adopt an amendment to the bylaws. A 100 percent fraction is equivalent to a unanimous vote of the votes cast. Some rules of organizations permit an 80 percent or 90 percent vote of the votes cast to adopt emergency measures.

There is a place and time for these various vote-counting protocols. but they must be used sparingly and with caution.

Double Majority of the Votes Cast

When an assembly consists of individual members and of caucuses, an organization may state, through its documents of authority, that a majority of the individual votes cast plus a majority of the caucus votes cast are required to adopt a proposal.

The double-majority vote-counting protocol is useful where constituent units within an organization have different voting strengths. For example, a delegation from California may have twenty-one votes, while one from Rhode Island may have two votes. If on a specific proposal the California delegation vote eighteen for and three against, while the Rhode Island delegation votes none for and two against, the total vote count is eighteen for and five against. At the second level of voting (the state level), it is one vote for (California) and one against (Rhode Island). In this way the smaller units are partly protected from the larger units.

The framers of the U.S. Constitution used an analogous vote-counting protocol by designing a bicameral Congress in which membership in the House of Representatives is based on population, giving the larger states more votes and therefore an advantage there. However, the Senate, if one considers it as the second level of voting, has two members per state, which somewhat offsets the advantage the larger states have in the House.

Double-majority votes often require two rounds of voting, because of the difficulty in distinguishing caucuses. The first vote is the individual vote, and the second vote is the caucus vote. To adopt a proposal requires adoption by a majority of the individual votes cast and adoption by a majority of the caucus votes cast. If a ballot vote is used, the caucus must be identified on the ballot to show how the caucus as a whole voted. The vote is recorded on a sheet designed to count individual votes and caucus votes. With electronic counting (using a keypad), the individual votes and caucus votes are counted automatically, and the results are displayed in seconds.

Other Protocols

Four other vote-counting protocols mentioned above are defined and explained through examples in chapter 11, "Nominations and Elections":

- Preferential voting

- The Borda count

- The Condorcet method

- Approval voting

These vote-counting protocols are useful when there are more than two options to select from. Although they may be used in other settings, they are especially useful in elections when there are more than two candidates.

Minimum Complement of Votes

In some jurisdictions there is a requirement that a defined minimum number of votes be cast in favor of a proposal for it to be adopted, provided the votes in favor exceed the votes against. This generally does not apply to elections, but it could. The purpose of this requirement is to ensure that meetings that barely meet quorum requirements or votes with many abstentions are fairly representative of the members.

The minimum complement of votes is calculated in different ways. The most common are:

- Majority of those present

- Majority of the entire membership

- Majority of the quorum

- Unanimity of those present

An example or two will suffice to explain the calculation of the minimum complement of votes. In a meeting assume 105 members are present. In the documents of authority, a quorum is defined as a hundred members present. A majority of the quorum is fifty-one (a majority of one hundred). This means that if the vote-counting protocol requires a majority of the quorum to adopt a proposal, fifty-one votes minimum must be cast in favor for it to be adopted. If a vote is taken and the vote is fifty for the proposal and thirty against, with twenty-five abstentions, the proposal is defeated.

If a board has twenty-four members present and the vote-counting protocol requires a majority of those present to adopt a proposal, all proposals require a minimum of thirteen votes to be adopted. A vote of twelve for and eleven against defeats the motion.

If the vote-counting protocol on a particular issue (say, removal of a member) requires all persons present to vote in favor of removal, the complement of votes required to adopt is the number present. In this situation a member who abstains while all others members vote in the affirmative in effect defeats the motion.

This is an important concept in decision making, as many jurisdiction and some organizations have now adopted such protocols to protect against unrepresentative decision making.

CHAPTER ELEVEN

~

Nominations and Elections

Definitions and Terms

- Election—The process of choosing a person for office or a position.
- Nominations—The process of choosing a person or persons to run in an election.
- Teller—A person who counts votes.
- Chief teller—The person in charge of the tellers.
- Tellers' report—A report identifying the vote count of an election. It includes such items as the total number of votes cast, the number of votes required for election, the number of votes cast for each candidate, and other items pertinent to determining the result of the election.
- Scrutineer—A person who witnesses the counting of votes on behalf of a candidate. A scrutineer has the authority to challenge the placement of individual votes for a candidate but does not have authority to decide the placement of the vote.
- Drawing Lots—An efficient method of breaking a tie in an election by randomly choosing the winner. This method may be used if it is included in a document of authority.
- Preferential voting—A voting system that requires a member to rank all candidates or choices on one ballot. This ranking, or preference listing, is then used to determine the winning candidate or proposal.

- Approval voting—Permits a member to cast a vote for as many candidates as are on the ballot. If there are five candidates, a voter may vote for one, two, three, four, or all five candidates, or none.
- Condorcet winner—A candidate who beats every other candidate in a pairwise, one-on-one contest.
- Borda count—A method of assigning numbers to a voters preference and then summing the numbers over all the voters to arrive at the winning candidate.

Nominations

The purpose of a nomination is to select formally a number of candidates who are qualified for a position or office. It is the preliminary to the appointment or election to a position or office. The candidates selected may be as few as one.

A candidate is required to be qualified in two respects. Firstly, the nominee must meet criteria contained in the documents of authority. If the documents of authority are silent, the fundamental criterion is that the nominee be a member of the organization. For other important positions, such as the presidency of an organization, other criteria may be stipulated regarding previous positions held, such as the number of years on the board. Secondly, the nominee should be selected on the basis of leadership qualities, experience, and other intrinsic qualities. This second dimension is what inspires an individual to vote for one candidate over another; it is the stuff of elections.

The method of nominating a person or persons for a position is as important as the election itself. It must be meticulously planned, be fair and be seen to be fair. The common nomination methods are:

- From the floor
- By committee
- By petition
- By the chair

Nominations from the Floor
This is the most frequent method of nominating candidates for a position. Nominations from the floor are always permitted, even when

other methods of nominations are specified in the documents of authority, unless specifically disallowed. For example, if an election process uses nominations by a nominating committee as the basis for obtaining candidates for positions, nominations from the floor are also permitted, unless the documents of authority prohibit them. It is generally not a good practice to disallow nominations from the floor. Members should be afforded the greatest flexibility in selecting their leaders. In addition, the method permits potential and future leaders to step forward and offer their talents and time to the organization.

If there is a nominating committee, nominations from the floor take place after the nominating committee has named its nominees for the position. Likewise, if the basis of nominating candidates is by petition, the petitioned candidates are first placed in nomination.

The rules for nominations from the floor are as follows:

- Members making nominations need not be recognized

- Nominations need not be seconded

- A nominee may decline the nomination at any time after being nominated but prior to the election

- A member may not nominate more nominees than there are places to be filled for the position

- A nominee need not be present to be nominated

- Nominations may be reopened by general consent or by a majority vote

Nomination by Committee

A nominations committee permits an organization to seek out the best candidates for office and ensures that at least one candidate is available to run for each position. The nominations committee is charged with finding competent individuals who are willing to serve and who meet the criteria for the various offices.

The membership of the nominations committee is best selected by the assembly as a whole. This avoids self-perpetuation of the leadership. The membership, at a meeting well in advance of the election meeting, elects the nominations committee as in any other election. As for any committee, there are various ways of selecting the members of the nominations committee; another option is a combination of board selection and membership selection; for instance, the board may appoint or elect the chair and the members elect the remainder of the members. In any case, the current leadership, in particular the president, must avoid any direct involvement with the nominations committee, either in appointing members to it or participating in the committee work. The president should be barred from participation in the nominations committee by a rule in the documents of authority.

The procedure by which the nominations committee goes about its work should be contained in the documents of authority. The general principles by which the nominations committee carries out its duties are:

- It selects the most competent candidate for each position.

- It may select more than one candidate for a position but is not required to do so.

- It casts a wide net throughout the organization in seeking nominees for each position.

- It rigorously stays within the candidate-qualification criteria defined for each position.

- It strictly follows the procedure or instructions defined in the documents of authority.

- It must obtain consent from a nominee to select that nominee for a position.

- It must present a report to the membership a reasonable time prior to the election meeting, either at another meeting or in the call to the election meeting.

- The nominations committee report contains, as a minimum, the names of the candidates, the objective qualifications of the candidate, and an indication of their willingness to run and to serve if elected.

- A minority report is not permitted from a member or members of the nominations committee.

- The committee may select one of its own members as a candidate.

The nominating committee report, or the slate of candidates selected by the committee, is not adopted by the membership. When the time arrives for nominations, the committee chair, or the chair's designate, names the committee's nominees as candidates for office.

Nomination by Petition

Nomination by petition is a common method of selecting nominees for office. It permits small groups of members to nominate a person for office. To be permitted, this method of nomination must be allowed by the documents of authority. The documents of authority must also describe the procedure by which a group of members may nominate. As a minimum the procedure must contain:

- The qualification of those persons who may submit a petition of nomination

- The number of qualified persons required to sign the petition of nomination

- The latest date by which the petition must be sent in

- The person or address to which the petition is to be submitted

The number of qualified persons required to sign the petition may be one person but is more often between two and ten. The date by which the petition is to be submitted should allow sufficient time for the names to be published to the membership.

Nominations by the Chair

This method of nomination is most expedient for the appointment of committee chairs and members of committees. It provides for an efficient nomination process. It also permits a chair, who is often the president of the organization, to nominate members who lean toward the policies of the administration. The right of the chair to make such nominations is contained in the documents of authority. It is understood that if the documents of authority give the chair the right to nominate, nominations from other members are not permitted.

This right of the chair to nominate is not to be confused with the right of the chair (or the president) to appoint. The right of the president to appoint must be defined in the documents of authority. That right may be limited to appointment of committee chairs or to committee members as well. The right may also be restricted by requiring ratification by the body. If the documents of authority are silent on the right of the chair or president to nominate or appoint, neither right exists.

In practice, nominations by the chair proceed as follows: The chair nominates one or more persons for a position; the body then proceeds to elect one of the nominees to the position. If for any reason no one is elected, the process is repeated, and the chair again nominates one or more candidates. The chair is not restricted as to whom may be nominated this second time.

Nominations Process at the Meeting

The nominations process for office is often carried out just prior to the election process. However it is good practice, if time permits, to nominate persons for office a day or more ahead of the election or to hold the nominations process in the morning and the election in the afternoon. This permits candidates to become better known to the electors and for the electors to study the candidates. It also allows the members an opportunity to find other candidates who are not on the nominating committee list.

It is good practice to nominate candidates for each position in turn. However, it is not wrong to open nominations for all positions at the same time. A person may be nominated for more than one position, provided they qualify for all the posts.

The nominations process is as follows:

1. The presiding officer declares nominations open: "Nominations are now open for the position of . . ."
2. If there is a nominations committee, the presiding officer or the chair of the nominations committee places the name(s) of its nominees on the nominations list. If nominations are by petition, the presiding officer places those nominees on the nominations list.
3. Nominations from the floor are then processed. Members, without being recognized, call out the name of their nominees. If the meeting is large, a rule may be instituted requiring nominators to

speak from a microphone. No second is required for a nomination. If a second is made, it is ignored. The presiding officer states, "Mr. Cole has been nominated for the position of . . ."

4. The presiding officer invites other nominees for the position.
5. When it is clear that no further nominations will be made, the presiding officer closes nominations without objection—"If there is no objection, nominations are closed [pause]. There being no objection, nominations are closed." If someone objects, the presiding officer must allow a reasonable time for the member to make a nomination. Nominations may also be closed by a majority vote.
6. Once nominations are closed, the presiding officer reads out the names of all nominees.
7. A common and useful practice is to permit the candidates, or their designees, a few minutes to speak on their candidatures.

Depending on the process for nominations and elections, the presiding officer either continues with nominations for the next position or proceeds to the election.

Elections

It is difficult to separate the methods of voting and elections. Elections use different physical methods of voting and different voting protocols to determine results. Common voting methods are covered in chapter 10. However, some voting methods are particularly useful for electing leaders of an organization. These methods may also be used to elect persons to committees, task forces, and other organizational groups. In addition, the methods described may also be used to select a subset of items from a number of proposals. For example, if a board or a committee were to select a short list of consultants, say three, from a list of ten, the election methods described below could be used. However, the following sections describe the concepts, principles and techniques of various election methods as they relate to electing members to office. It is left to the reader to extend the concepts and principles to other situations in which social choices are made.

The two main principles of elections are:

- The members' right to information

- Courtesy and respect for all participants

These principles are consistent with the principles of parliamentary law and democracy. An organization's election procedure should ensure that these two principles guide the overall process.

If the documents of authority are silent on elections, the rules are:

- A majority of votes cast elects

- Ballot voting is used

- If for any reason there is "no election," all candidates remain on the ballot (candidates cannot be dropped)

- Not only is the result of the election announced, but each of the individual count tallies is announced

- A person need not be nominated to be elected

- Any member who meets the qualifying criteria to be a candidate has a right to run for office

- Candidates must have access to the electorate, and the electorate must have access to the candidates

To be permissible, any variation from the above rules must be provided for in the documents of authority. For example, if it is desired that the candidate with the lowest vote be dropped from the subsequent ballot when there is "no election," that must be specified in a document of authority. Similarly, if only persons nominated are to be eligible to win an election, that rule must be included in a document of authority, phrased in such a way that a write-in candidate could not win the election.

Elections may be characterized by the participants in the election process and the methods of election. The "methods of elections" are the physical methods of casting a vote, described in chapter 10, and the various vote-counting protocols, also introduced in chapter 10. The participants in elections are:

- The candidates

- The voters

- The tellers committee

- The scrutineers

Candidates

A *candidate* is a person qualified for office who has been nominated for office. A *write-in candidate* is a person who, though not nominated, receives at least one vote in an election. It is not necessary that a person be nominated to be elected. Any member may vote for any other member— qualified or unqualified, nominated or not nominated—and have their vote counted. If an unqualified person (or a fictitious character) attains a majority of the votes required to elect, there is no election, and a reballot is required.

All candidates are permitted the greatest flexibility in promoting their candidacies to the electorate. The rules should permit the candidates to describe their credentials in material circulated as part of the call to the meeting, in the organization's newsletter, in all-candidates meetings, and in leaflets distributed at or before the meeting. A combination of these methods of communicating, some of which are funded by the organization, must be available to all candidates. The rights of candidates are contained in the documents of authority.

At the meeting, candidates or their designee are permitted a short period of time to address the members, either during the nominations process or just prior to the election. If the documents of authority are silent on this right, a five-minute speech is permitted. The candidates must address their credentials for office and shall not attack other candidates or their credentials.

The Voters

All members of an organization or body have an inherent right to vote in the election of candidates for office. There are some exceptions:

- A member who is not present may not vote unless the documents of authority permit proxy voting, mail-in voting, or some other method of voting at a distance.

- Certain classes of memberships may be restricted in voting, through the documents of authority.

- Members may be disciplined by suspension of their right to vote. Such a person is considered "a member not in good standing."

The most crucial aspect of elections is the accurate identification of those entitled to vote. Concomitantly, it is very important that measures be taken to inhibit from voting those not entitled to vote. The first step in ensuring accuracy of the voting list is preparation by the credentials committee of a list of registered voters (see "Credential Committee," chapter 12). The credentials committee should also distribute the voting cards during member registration.

Tellers Committee

The tellers committee is charged with counting votes, collecting ballots when a ballot vote is taken, and reporting the count to the assembly. The tellers committee does not report the result to the assembly; only the presiding officer does so. Additional duties that the tellers committee may be given include counting the assembly during a quorum check and distributing ballots when a ballot vote is ordered by the assembly.

The presiding officer appoints the tellers committee, designating one member as chair. The committee takes no action unless instructed by the presiding officer—"The tellers will now distribute the ballots"; "The polls are closed, and the tellers will retire and count the votes"; "The tellers shall now report."

When the voting protocol is a majority of the votes cast, the report of the tellers committee is as given in table 11.1.

Table 11.1. Report of the Tellers—Majority of Votes Cast

Number of votes cast	210
Votes required for election	106
Christine Kay	121
Ron Rzepka	47
Neil John	39
Votes not allocated:	
Marked incorrectly (voted for two candidates)	2
Votes for ineligible person (fictitious character)	1
Illegal votes	0

If the voting protocol is a majority of those voters present, the tellers' report is adjusted to read as in table 11.2. The remainder of the report would remain the same.

During the count of the ballots the chief teller should monitor the overall counting process but refrain from participating in the count. If there is disagreement on the disposition of a particular ballot that is not resolved by the end of the counting process, the disagreement must be reported to the assembly by a notation on the tellers' report. The tellers must agree unanimously on the disposition of contested or illegible ballots. The assembly need not take any action on any disagreement noted on the tellers' report.

The tellers ignore any blank ballots, bring to the attention of the chief teller any vote that they are unable to correlate to a candidate, and report any suspicious ballots, such as multiple ballots folded together. Minor spelling mistakes (usually for write-in candidates) or variations in check marks do not invalidate a ballot, provided the teller is sure to which candidate the vote should go. Any suspicious ballot that the committee believes is cast by an illegal voter is reported on the tellers' report and is not counted in the number of votes cast or in determining the votes required to elect.

When reporting, the chair of the committee reads the tellers' report verbatim and hands the report to the presiding officer. The presiding officer rereads the report and announces the result. If the report of the tellers committee is complex—for instance, if the assembly is electing six directors from twenty candidates—the chair of the committee should confer with the presiding officer and, if appropriate, present the tellers' report in order, from the highest vote attained to the lowest vote attained, in addition to the order on the ballot. This complication also occurs when there are many write-in votes.

Using the same example of six to elect, if not all six are elected, a reballot will be required. Only candidates on the original ballot remain on the ballot, although nominations may be reopened by majority vote.

Table 11.2. Adjusted Tellers' Report—Majority of Voters Present

Number of votes present	214
Number of votes cast	210
Votes required for election	108

Scrutineers

Scrutineers may be appointed by candidates to ensure the integrity of the election and that their interests are protected. A scrutineer attends the vote count with the tellers committee and is allowed to see each marked ballot. A scrutineer only observes the count and in no circumstances is permitted to handle a ballot box or ballot or to participate in the count. The scrutineer may challenge the allocation of a ballot during the count, but only the tellers committee decides on the final allocation. A scrutineer who interferes with the counting process or becomes abusive may be removed from the room where the count is taking place. The scrutineer is not permitted to report to the presiding officer or to the assembly.

Example: A Typical Election

A typical election might proceed in this way:

Presiding officer: "The election for the office of secretary is now open. A majority vote of the votes cast is required to elect. Please use the blue ballot, which has the word "Secretary" at the top. There are three nominated candidates: Mr. Shaw, Ms. McNeil, and Mrs. Noble. Mr. Henderson was nominated from the floor; please write in his name in the fourth slot on the ballot. To vote for one of these four candidates, please mark your ballot clearly with an X or a check mark. Mark the ballot for one candidate only. Marking the ballot for more than one candidate will spoil the ballot. When you have marked the ballot, deposit it in the ballot box at the front of the room. The polls are now open for the position of secretary."

Presiding officer: "Have all who wish to cast their vote for secretary done so? [pause] If there is no objection, the polls will be closed. [pause] There being no objection, the polls are now closed. The tellers shall retire to count the vote."

Presiding officer: "The tellers have now returned from counting, and I recognize the chief teller, Mr. Kumar, to report."

Chief teller: "The tellers' report is as follows: number of votes cast, sixty-three; votes required to elect, thirty-two; James Shaw, twenty-nine; Peg Noble, twenty-one; Helen McNeil, eight; Bruce Henderson, five; illegal votes, none. All votes were allocated as cast, and none were spoiled."

Presiding officer: Repeats the chief tellers' report and announces, "No candidate received the required number of votes for election. Please use the burgundy ballot [holds up the burgundy ballot], which is located at the end of your ballot slips. Mark the ballot at the top with the word 'Secretary.' Please write on your ballot your choice of candidate for the office of secretary. The names of the nominated candidates are on the screen—James Shaw, Peg Noble, Helen McNeil, and Bruce Henderson. Are there any questions? There being no questions, the polls are again open for the office of secretary."

When one of the candidates is elected, the presiding officer, after reading the tellers' report, announces, "James Shaw has been elected as secretary of the association." The presiding officer then continues with other positions open for election.

Example: Elect Five from Eleven Nominations

This next example assumes that nine nominations have been received prior to the meeting by petition, that nominations from the floor and write-ins for other members are allowed, that a majority is required to elect, that dropping candidates from the ballot is not permitted, and that the members are to elect five positions.

Presiding officer: "The election for the board of directors is now open. To be elected, candidates must attain a majority of the ballots cast. Please use the pink ballot that has the phrase "Directors—Five to Elect" at the top. There are nine nominated candidates. These have been listed on the ballot in the order in which the nominations were received." [Presiding officer reads the list of nine candidates]. "Are there any nominations from the floor?"

Member: "I nominate Mr. Ashok Khera as a candidate."

Presiding officer: "Mr. Ashok Khera's name has been placed in nomination for the board of directors. Are there any further nominations?"

Member: "I nominate Ms. Kathy Morelli as a candidate."

Presiding officer: "Ms. Kathy Morelli's name has been placed in nomination for the board of directors. Are there any further nominations? [pause] I do not see anyone approaching the microphone. If there are no objections, nominations will be closed. [pause] There being no objections, nominations are closed. Please write Ashok Khera's name in the tenth slot in the ballot and immediately below that, Kathy Morelli's name. We now have eleven candidates for five director positions.

"You may mark your ballot for up to five candidates. If you mark it for more than five candidates, the ballot will be spoiled. Please mark it clearly with an X or a check mark. When you have marked the ballot, deposit it in the ballot box at the front of the room. The polls are now open for the five director positions."

Presiding officer: "Have all who wish to cast their vote for the director position done so? [pause]. If there is no objection, the polls will be closed. [pause] There being no objection, the polls are now closed. The tellers shall take the ballot boxes and retire to count the vote."

Presiding officer: "The tellers have now returned from counting and I recognize the chief teller, Mr. Bell, to report."

Chief teller: "The tellers' report is as follows: number of votes cast (ballots) 205; votes required to elect, 103; Ann Sprague, thirty-one; Bert Logan, 140; John McCartney, twelve; Mohammed Elgazar, 113; Dot Friend, ninety-five; Daniel Taggart, ninety-one; Fran DiSilva, 140; Richard Li, seventy-four; Tom Long, thirty; Ashok Khera, 101; Kathy Morelli, eighty-nine; Paul Docherty (write-in), four; Bret Simms (write-in), one. Votes not allocated included one marked incorrectly (voted for all candidates); there were no illegal votes. That is the report of the tellers committee, Mr. President."

Presiding officer (repeats the chief tellers' report and announces): "Three candidates have received a majority of the votes cast and are elected to the board of directors. They are Bert Logan, Mohammed Elgazar, and Fran DiSilva. The members must now elect two candidates from the remaining eight persons who have been nominated. The eight candidates have been listed on the overhead projector.

"Please use the white ballot, which has been marked with "Director Position" [holds up the white ballot], which is located at the end of your ballot slips. Please write on this ballot up to two names as your choice of candidate for the office of director. If you mark your ballot with more than two names, the ballot will be spoiled, and its votes will not be allocated to any candidate. The names of the nominated candidates are on the screen. Are there any questions? There being no questions, the polls are again open for you to cast your ballot for the two director positions."

Chief teller (when all ballots have been cast, the polls closed, and the vote counted): "Number of votes cast (ballots), 201; votes required to elect, 101; Ann Sprague, eleven; John McCartney, ten; Dot Friend, 103; Daniel Taggart, 105; Richard Li, twenty; Tom Long, four; Ashok Khera, 121; Kathy Morelli, sixteen; Paul Docherty (write-in), six. Votes not allocated include two marked incorrectly (voted for more than two candidates); there were no illegal votes. That is the report of the tellers committee, Mr. President."

Presiding officer: "The remaining two director positions have been filled. I declare Mr. Daniel Taggart and Mr. Ashok Khera elected to the board of directors."

Electing a Number of Candidates from a Greater Number of Nominees

There are some unique rules associated with electing a number of candidates from a greater number of nominations, as occurred in the second example above. One of these rules is highlighted in the example—on the second ballot, three candidates actually attained a majority (Taggart, Khera, and Friend). When this occurs, the two candidates with the highest number of votes are elected.

A second rule, not illustrated above, is that if Friend and Taggart, in the example, had each received, say, 104 votes, the fifth-place position would not have been filled, and a third ballot would have been required, with all candidates remaining on the ballot, unless the documents of authority stated otherwise. The default is that all candidates remain on the ballot.

If the top two candidates each attain a majority and have the same number of votes, both are declared elected to the position of director, and a reballot is not required. If there happens to be a distinction between the fourth and fifth position (for example, the fourth position is for a term of two years while the fifth position is for one year), the default is that lots are drawn for the fourth and fifth positions in the event of a tie.

One other feature of electing a number of candidates from a greater number of nominations is that members need not cast votes for all the positions open. A voter may actually cast a vote for anything up to the number of positions open. This means that the number of ballots cast is the determining factor in the vote required to elect, not the number of votes cast for all candidates. This may lead to voting strategy, whereby a member casts a vote for only one candidate; this is called "bullet voting." Some organizations disallow bullet voting through their documents of authority. When disallowed, a ballot cast with less than the required votes marked is consider spoiled and is not allocated to any candidate.

Preferential Voting

The preferential vote-counting protocol is useful when voting by mail and when there is no opportunity to reballot or the cost of reballoting is prohibitively high. In a meeting setting, this type of voting should not be required, provided that the organizers leave enough time to re-ballot. A reballot is preferred, as it permits the members to gauge support for each candidate.

There are many preferential vote-counting protocols. They all have the characteristic of only requiring one ballot to be cast and using second, third, and further choices to proceed iteratively toward a majority vote for a candidate or candidates (if there is more than one position to elect). They also require last-place candidates (sometimes more) to be dropped and their votes distributed to other candidates. It is considered a more efficient way of voting, as only one ballot is cast, but depending on the complexity of transferring votes when candidates are dropped, the counting process itself is prone to error. With computers, the error factor can readily be overcome.

The preferential vote-counting protocol itself uses a majority of the votes cast as the basis to elect. It permits the voter to rank the candidates in the voters' preferred order. If there are five candidates of which one is to be elected, the voter may rank all candidates from one to five, with "one" being the preferred choice and "five" the least preferred. On the first ballot, all first-place votes for each candidate are determined and reported. If any candidate receives a majority of the votes cast, that candidate is elected, and the election is concluded. If, however, no candidate is elected, the candidate with the least number of votes is dropped, and that candidate's second-place votes are redistributed to the other candidates. The first-place votes and the redistributed votes are counted for the four remaining candidates. If a majority of votes cast is now attained by a candidate, that candidate is declared elected. If a majority has not been attained, the new last-place candidate is dropped, and the votes are again redistributed. This redistribution again takes the second-place votes of the new last-place candidate and places their second choice—or if the new last-place candidate's second choice has been eliminated previously, then the third choice—on the three remaining candidates. This process is repeated until one candidate attains a majority.

On the first count, if two or more candidates have the least number of votes, lots are drawn to determine which candidate is to be eliminated. If on subsequent counts (after redistributing votes) two or more candidates have the least number of votes, the candidate having the least number of votes on the previous count, or counts, is eliminated. In the unlikely event the candidates are tied all the way back to the first count, lots are drawn to eliminate a candidate. If two candidates remain and the count is tied, the previous count, or counts, are used to determine the final result. The candidate with the most votes in the previous count (or counts) is declared the winner.

If a voter does not rank all candidates and (in the extreme) selects only one candidate, that voter's ballot cannot be redistributed when the candidate is eliminated. In this case the ballot is considered exhausted. The exhausted ballot is set aside and is not considered in any further counting. There is thus no advantage to the voter in voting only for a single favorite candidate. The counting may be complex, so the tellers committee should be carefully selected for accuracy in counting and recording numbers.

To give an example of preferential voting, let us assume that one person is to be elected from six candidates. A simplified tellers' report for preferential voting would be as shown in table 11.3. The presiding officer, after reading the tellers committee report, declares Candidate A elected.

Table 11.3. Preferential Voting—Simplified Teller's Report

Number of ballots cast		460			
Votes required to elect		231			
	1st count	2nd count	3rd count	4th count	5th count
Candidate A	111	111	131	180	250
Candidate B	10	drop			
Candidate C	103	105	115	120	drop
Candidate D	130	132	138	152	192
Candidate E	60	66	74	drop	
Candidate F	46	46	drop		
Totals	460	460	458	452	442
Votes exhausted			2	6	10
Number of ballots not allocated		0			
Number of illegal votes		0			
Number of total ballots exhausted		18			

Election Paradoxes

In April 1999 the author published an article entitled "Election Paradoxes" in the American Institute of Parliamentarian's *Parliamentary Journal*, volume 60, no. 2. The article was written to highlight potential problems in elections when there are three or more candidates running for office. The article also introduced a number of students of the subject who have recognized certain paradoxes that arise during elections, and described their methods for overcoming the problems involved. This section repeats the example used in the article.

The essence of the example is drawn from the work of Dr. Donald Saari, then of the Department of Mathematics, Northwestern University, now at the University of California, Irvine. It shows the plurality method of voting to be one of worst forms of determining the result of an election. The example and analysis also introduces in a concrete way the Borda count, the Condorcet winner, and approval voting as alternative vote-counting protocols.

Assume there are three candidates—Ann, Bill, and Charles. There are twelve voters (A through L), who rank the candidates as shown in table 11.4.

Table 11.4. An Apparent Paradox

	A	B	C	D	E	F	G	H	I	J	K	L
Ann	1	1	1	1	1	3	3	3	3	3	3	3
Bill	2	2	2	2	2	2	2	2	2	1	1	1
Charles	3	3	3	3	3	1	1	1	1	2	2	2

Using plurality as the vote-counting protocol, the result is Ann five, Charles four, and Bill three. Ann would be elected. However, if before the election Charles dropped out, we would have a one-on-one election. The result would be that Bill would have seven votes and Ann five. Bill would be elected. Now consider Ann dropping out; Bill would go one on one with Charles. This time Bill gets eight votes and Charles five votes. Again Bill, would be elected.

So we have the paradox that the person (Bill) who finished last in the plurality vote would actually defeat the other two candidates one on one. Bill is the Condorcet winner, as he beats both other candidates one on one.

To take this further, if Bill drops out, Charles would get seven votes and Ann five votes. Charles would be elected. The person (Ann) who finished first in the plurality vote actually loses to both other candidates in one-on-one voting. She is also bottom-ranked by a majority of the voters.

This apparent paradox occurs because by taking account only of the voters first choices we never learn their second and third choices. This loss of information leads to anomalous results. The example of the 1991 gubernatorial race in Louisiana described in chapter 10 is a prime example of what can result from plurality voting.

Returning to table 11.4 and the election between Ann, Bill, and Charles, let us play a mind game. Suppose the instructions to the twelve voters had been confusing and that instead of ranking their preference in a first-second-third order, the voters had thought they were to rank the candidates in order of preference—third, second, and first. So let us remake the table so that if Ann is ranked first, that really means third, and if she is ranked third, that really means first. Of course, second would remain second. The new table would be as in table 11.5.

Table 11.5   An Apparent Paradox—New Ranking

	A	B	C	D	E	F	G	H	I	J	K	L
Ann	3	3	3	3	3	1	1	1	1	1	1	1
Bill	2	2	2	2	2	2	2	2	2	3	3	3
Charles	1	1	1	1	1	3	3	3	3	2	2	2

Lo and behold, table 11.5 shows that the plurality result would still have Ann as the winner. The result is Ann seven, Charles five, and Bill none. So even though the voters gave exactly the opposite preferences in their individual votes, they still elect Ann under the plurality method of making the group choice. It appears that Ann comes out a winner no matter how the voters vote. This is indeed a paradox. This time Ann would also be the Condorcet winner, as she defeats both Bill and Charles one on one.

Referring to table 11.4 again, is it fair that Ann should win? She would certainly lose on one-on-one elections against Bill and Charles. On one level, the fairest result and the "correct" group decision would be to have Bill the winner. Would a runoff election produce a better result? In most runoffs, the candidate with the least votes drops from the ballot; Bill would drop from the ballot, leaving Ann and Charles facing each other, one on one. As shown earlier, Charles wins seven to five.

So we have the situation in table 11.4, where Ann wins with plurality counting, Bill wins with Condorcet counting (pairwise), and Charles wins on a runoff method of counting.

Is There a Better Way?

Approval Voting
One method of voting that has gained some support is *approval voting*. This gives the voter one vote for each of the candidates. If there are ten candidates the voter has ten votes and may spread them around the candidates of whom he or she approves. The voter may still only cast one vote per candidate.

From table 11.4, if we assume that each voter has three votes (there are three candidates) and that each of them approves of two candidates only, then approval voting yields the result Bill twelve, Charles seven, and Ann five. Note that Bill receives twelve votes because every voter in table 11.4 has Bill as either first or second choice.

One criticism leveled against approval voting is that it tends to benefit centrist candidates, who may have broader appeal, over extreme candidates. The method is also open to "strategic voting" wherein a candidate's supporters approve only of their own candidate, by casting one vote instead of perhaps two or three votes to take in second and third choices. Note that approval voting degenerates to plurality voting when all supporters vote strategically and vote only for their own candidates.

Approval voting has merit within voluntary associations, such as the American Statistical Association and the Institute of Management Science, which in fact use the method. In voluntary associations, careers are not normally at stake, and members are likely to vote their true preferences and avoid strategic or insincere voting. This makes approval voting a viable option for voluntary associations. However, approval voting is unlikely to prove effective in a truly political arena where sides are far apart.

The Borda Count Method

Professor Saari, although he admits it is still not perfect, in light of Kenneth Arrow's "Impossibility Theorem" (see below), believes that the Borda count method gives the best overall method for arriving at the group's decision after individuals have voted their preferences. The mathematical analysis supporting this conclusion is provided in his articles and books, which are listed as references. The Borda count assigns numbers to a voter's preferences and sums the numbers over all the voters to arrive at the winning candidate.

If we assume in table 11.4 that a first place gets two points, a second place one point, and the third place candidate gets zero points, the result using the Borda count method is Bill fifteen points, Charles eleven points, and Ann ten points. Saari opines that the Borda count is a natural extension of what is done in one-on-one elections (otherwise known as pairwise, or Condorcet, elections). He has shown that the Borda count achieves the "fairness" goal of elections. Note that in table 11.4, as shown earlier, Bill would also win the one-on-one elections.

The Borda count is analogous to the way in which the educational system selects its best students. If Ann, as a student, got five As and seven Fs, and Bill gets three As and nine Bs, which is the better student? Probably Bill is. Our educational system, then, uses the Borda count intuitively, yet for hundreds of years Western democracies have been selecting leaders through the plurality system of voting, which has been discredited for just as long.

Summary

There is no perfect way of turning individual voting preferences into group decisions when there are more than two candidates. This does not mean that we give up on voting but that we must strive for a better method, now that we know the limitations of various voting methods. Donald Saari has shown that plurality voting is probably the worst form of all voting methods and that the voting method that best approaches the elusive "fairness" principle is the Borda count method. Approval voting should be considered as an expedient method for voluntary associations, but its usefulness depends on the culture of the organization and the degree of politicization of its membership.

Many Historical Figures Have Analyzed Voting Methods:
- The Marquis de Condorcet, 1743–1794—A scientist of the European Enlightenment period. Appointed by Louis XVI as inspector general of the French mint (1774), in 1777 he was appointed secretary of the Académie des Sciences. He is famous for the "Condorcet Paradox," which showed that under certain circumstances when A wins a majority over B and B wins a majority over C, it does not necessarily follow that A beats C.
- J. C. Borda, 1733–1799—A contemporary and rival of Condorcet. Recognizing also the existence of paradoxes in election results, he championed the Borda count as a method of overcoming anomalies. His main pursuit was the mathematics of fluids, and he was one of the driving forces in the spread of the decimal system.
- Kenneth Arrow—The Joan Kenney Professor of Economics and professor of operations research at Stanford University. In 1972, he received the Nobel Prize in economic science. He received the 1986

Von Neumann Theory Prize for his work on general economic equilibrium. In 1952 he showed, through his "Impossibility Theorem," that given any voting procedure, for three or more candidates there will be some set of individual voter preferences that violates the principle of fairness in elections.

• Donald Saari—Professor of mathematics at the University of California, Irvine, has written many books and article on social choices, particularly on election paradoxes. He is known for his vast theoretical knowledge of the mathematics involved in turning individual choices into group decisions. He has applied this knowledge to the real world of elections.

Further Reading

Arrow, K.J. *Social Choice and Individual Values.* 2nd ed. (New York: Wiley, 1963). This book, which explains the Impossibility Theorem, is considered a classic in the field.

McLean, I. "The Borda and Condorcet principles." *Social Choice and Welfare* 7(2) (1990): 99–108. Both the Borda and Condorcet principles are explored and explained.

McLean I., and F. Hewitt, eds. *Condorcet: Foundations of Social Choice and Political Theory.* (Cheltenham, U.K.: Edward Elgar, 1995). The original writings of Condorcet.

Saari, D. G. *The Borda Dictionary.* (Heidelberg, Ger.: Social Choice and Welfare, 1991). All of the properties of the Borda count are described in this article.

——— *Basic Geometry of Voting.* (Heidelberg, Ger.: Springer-Verlag, 1994). The basic mathematics behind voting paradoxes are described.

——— *Chaotic Elections! A Mathematician Looks at Voting.* (American Mathematical Society, 2001). A popularization of *Basic Geometry of Voting,* with application to current events.

CHAPTER TWELVE

~

Annual Meetings
and Conventions

Committees and procedures are important structural aspects of an association's annual meeting or convention. This chapter does not go into the myriad of details involved in an association's most exciting and most important meeting of the year, but it tries to provide the framework of committees, their duties, and how they work.

Members go to annual meetings for many reasons. They meet friends, get a boost of adrenalin for their favorite association, and get educated; some actually go to conduct the business of the association. This last may be considered boring by many meeting goers, but most agree that it is very important to get the business aspects right. If the association is incorporated, the law requires that it be done right.

There is a distinction between an *annual meeting* of an association and an *annual convention* of an association. The convention assembly comprises delegates who represent defined segments of membership, usually geographic, while the annual meeting is composed of individual members who attend and vote at the regular meetings. The distinction is becoming blurred, in that some associations hold annual conventions at which the attendees are not representative delegates but are individual members themselves. Likewise, annual meetings sometimes involve delegates.

From a procedural point of view, the distinction between a delegate assembly and one of individual members mainly impacts voting structure. A delegate assembly may consist of various caucuses with different voting strengths. For example, the voting strength of a caucus group is most often based on the numbers of individual members who belong to its constituency, which in turn is generally geographic, based on entities such as counties, states, or provinces. In an international association, caucuses may be based on countries.

Where individual members make up the assembly, each individual has one vote; where delegates make up the assembly, each delegate may hold a number of votes. Because of this difference, the bylaws of the association need to define:

- The caucus division on which the delegate system is based

- The process for determining the number of votes a caucus division may hold

- The number of delegates who may represent a caucus division

- How delegates may be appointed or elected

- How alternate delegates may be appointed or elected

- Any other provision associated with the delegate system of representation

Whether the annual meeting is based on individual votes or delegate votes, the work of the assembly is the same. The work is, as a minimum, to:

1. Hear the reports of the officers.
2. Hear the reports of standing committees.
3. Conduct elections of officer, board and other important positions.
4. Hear the report of the auditor.
5. Conduct other business as may properly come before the meeting.

The annual meeting or convention usually consists of three groups of activities:

- Business meeting
- Educational topics
- Social events

The annual meeting program or convention program comprises all of these items, meticulously planned and timed. This book is mainly concerned about the business meeting, and that is the focus of the remainder of this chapter.

For clarity, the remainder of this chapter will use the term "convention" in preference to the "annual meeting," but the same concepts and rules apply in either case.

Business Meeting Agenda

The agenda for the business meeting of a convention is usually contained in the documents of authority. Chapter 3 defines a standard order of business of an association, but each association would be wise to define an order of business for its business meetings that meets its own needs. Certain aspects of the meeting should be timed, as business is usually intertwined with other aspects of the overall program, such as educational and social events that occur throughout the meeting. Timed events would normally include:

- Registration of members or delegates
- When the business meeting starts
- When the business meeting is expected to adjourn
- Nomination of officers and election of officers
- Any controversial topic that will be dealt with during the business meeting

Indicating times on the agenda, at least for the above-listed items, permits members to organize their time around important events that occur during the convention.

Convention Committees

Because of the importance of the annual convention and the complexity of its organization, four committees in particular must operate efficiently and effectively:

- Credentials committee

- Convention rules committee

- Program committee

- Reference committee

Credentials Committee
This committee reports shortly after the meeting is called to order. It establishes the quorum for the business meeting and establishes that the body of delegates represents the association in assembly.

The credentials committee is to accredit each delegate or member as a voting member of the assembly, furnishing badges and voting credentials. The committee maintains an up-to-date list of all voting delegates, the *official registered voters list*. Because some delegates and members will register late, the committee may be required to report more than once. It should always be required to report prior to elections and bylaw amendments, in order to establish an accurate count of votes and thereby ensure the credibility of the meeting.

The chair of the credentials committee reports as follows:

Madam President, the credentials committee reports that as of 8:45 A.M. Friday, 12 April, 2002, there are ninety-five delegates registered, representing 1,255 votes. There are eighty-nine alternate delegates present. The attached official registered voters list provides a breakdown of the delegates and the number of votes each holds. On behalf of the credentials committee, I move the adoption of the credentials report.

No second is required.

Before taking the vote, the presiding officer asks, "Are there any questions on the credentials report? [pause] There are no questions. This vote requires a majority to adopt. All those in favor of adopting the credentials report say 'aye.' [pause] Those opposed say 'no.' [pause] The ayes have it, and the report of the credentials committee is adopted."

With the adoption of the credentials report, the body is properly established.

In some associations, delegates may be contested. If such a case arises, an accredited delegate may bring it to the attention of the assembly. A motion to substitute one delegate, or group of delegates, by another delegate or group is in order. A motion made to substitute delegates requires a second, is debatable, and requires a majority vote to adopt. The contested delegates, if already accredited, are permitted to vote. The delegates bringing the contest are permitted to make their case but are not permitted to vote.

Convention Rules Committee

The convention rules committee reports after the credentials committee. The rules committee's mandate is to propose special rules of order and administrative policy (policy is described in chapter 2) for use during the convention. Often the same rules are used from year to year, but they should be adopted afresh each time. This provides an opportunity for delegate or members to add new rules or amend existing ones.

The convention rules proposed are often a mixture of special rules of order (that substitute for rules contained in the parliamentary authority) and administrative rules for the convention. For example, a special rule of order might allow each delegate or member to speak only once, for three minutes, on any given motion. Such a rule would depart from this book—which permits, as a default, members to speak twice for five minutes. An administrative rule might be that delegates or members must wear their badges at all times while in the meeting area.

A two-thirds vote is required to adopt convention rules. Subsequent to this vote, individual administrative rules require only a majority to adopt or amend; rules of order continue to require a two-thirds vote to adopt or amend. If a convention rule of order is rescinded, the associated rule contained in the parliamentary authority returns to effect.

When reporting, the chair of the committee reads the proposed convention rules and says, "On behalf of the rules committee, I propose the adoption of the convention rules just read." A member may propose an amendment to the rules. An amendment to the rules, prior to their adoption, requires a majority vote to adopt.

The presiding officer then says, "The motion is on the adoption of the convention rules. This motion requires a two-thirds vote to adopt. All those in favor of adopting the convention rules say 'aye.' [pause] Those opposed say 'no.' [pause] The ayes have it, and the convention rules are adopted."

A typical set of convention rules is listed in appendix D.

Program Committee
The program committee reports after the rules committee and may report thereafter at frequent intervals as required to keep the delegates and members informed. The program committee is charged with organizing all aspects of the convention program—business, educational, and social. It is often a complex task; there may be hundreds or even thousands of attendees, and a program spanning three or more days. The work of this committee is the most time-consuming of any committee, in that it may start a year or more prior to the event, when facilities have to be arranged, contracts signed, members informed, progress reported to the board, hotel rooms allocated, transportation arranged, and social events planned. The program committee is often divided into other subcommittees to look after key areas of convention planning.

The program committee report presents the latest program to the delegates for adoption. Often programs are printed weeks ahead of the convention; the committee may in its report present amendments to the program previously distributed; if not, the chair reports, "Mr. President, each delegate upon registration has been furnished with an up-to-date copy of the convention program. On behalf of the committee, I propose the adoption of the convention program as distributed." The presiding officer asks if there are any questions and then takes the vote on the convention program: "All in favor of adopting the convention program as distributed say 'aye.' [pause] Those opposed say 'no.' [pause] The ayes have it, and the convention program is adopted as distributed."

Reference Committees

The purpose of a reference committee is to examine all resolutions and main motions that are planned to come before the convention and recommend their disposition. Large conventions, which may have many resolutions proposed, often have a number of reference committees. For example, there may be reference committees on bylaws, education, or legislation. Each of them is given the resolutions or main motions that pertain to its area; all resolutions on education, for instance, would be sent to the reference committee on education.

The reference committee meets to discuss the many resolutions that it has been given. If necessary, it contacts the initiators of resolutions for clarification or further information. The committee may, depending on its authority, combine or reword resolutions.

The reference committee holds a reference committee hearing, as part of its work during the convention, at which it presents to the members in attendance each resolution that has been assigned to it. The date and time of the reference committee hearing is published, and all members are invited to participate. At the hearing the reference committee opens each resolution to debate and inquiry. Any member in attendance may speak to each resolution at least once. Those who initiated resolutions would explain their rationales; other members may advocate or oppose resolutions. Members may make recommendations to improve specific resolutions. No substantive votes are taken at a hearing; the main purpose is to listen to the opinions pro and con on each resolution.

The hearing is conducted under rules published by the reference committee. It is not good practice for the reference committee members to advocate any position on a resolution; it should limit itself to providing facts and background to those attending the hearing. The reference committee members will have their own say when they meet again, behind closed doors, to adopt committee positions on each resolution. The normal disposition for a resolution is either to "defeat," "adopt," or "refer to committee." In some instances, the committee may recommend amendments, in which case it would present the resolution to the assembly with that amendment.

The reference committee may place noncontroversial resolutions and others that it believes have general support, as gathered from the hearing, on a consent agenda "for adoption." It may also place resolutions that it believes do not have support on a consent agenda "for rejection." The consent agenda concept (see chapter 3) allows the reference committee to dispose of many such resolutions with one vote. This is important if there are many reference committees or many resolutions to be processed. However, any member may withdraw any item on demand from the reference committee's consent agenda.

When the reference committee reports to the assembly, it first presents its consent agenda "for adoption." The presiding officer asks the members in assembly if anyone wishes to remove a resolution from the consent agenda. If any member does, there is no discussion or vote on the removal; the affected resolution is placed with the resolutions that will be dealt with separately. The presiding officer then takes the vote on the consent agenda en bloc. The consent agenda "for rejection" is then processed. A member may remove a resolution from the consent agenda "for rejection" and place it with those that will be dealt with separately.

The wording used by the presiding officer when dealing with the adoption of consent agenda "for rejection" is important. The presiding officer should say, "Shall the agenda 'for rejection' be adopted? The reference committee recommends that you vote 'aye' on this motion. All in favor say 'aye.' [pause] Those against say 'no.' [pause] The ayes [noes] have it, and the consent agenda 'for rejection' is adopted [lost]." The assembly must understand the meaning of an 'aye' and 'no' vote in these circumstances. Essentially, the members, by voting 'aye,' defeat all motions on the consent agenda "for rejection."

The reference committee then presents each of the remaining resolutions, indicating its recommendation on each. The presiding officer assumes the motion in each case, saying, "Having in mind the recommendation of the reference committee, the motion before you is . . . " The motion or resolution is dealt with like all other main motions that come before the assembly.

CHAPTER THIRTEEN

~

Questions and Answers

A parliamentary authority cannot answer every question that may arise. The fundamental rules of parliamentary law listed and described in chapter 1 of this book may be used as a basis from which to derive satisfactory and defendable answers. However, that may not be enough; the bylaws and other documents of authority that the organization has adopted may govern the situation. To complicate matters, civil law sometimes dictates procedure, in which case the organization's counsel may become involved.

However, the answers this chapter provides are right for most cases; they are certainly right in terms of this parliamentary authority. However any answer to a parliamentary problem must be tested against the organization's documents of authority. The following questions are from the experience of the author; they are typically asked of the author in his role as parliamentarian or meeting consultant.

Should a committee's report be adopted when it is presented?

A committee's report should not be adopted verbatim unless the intention is to publish the report outside the organization. Reports often contain supporting material (facts, preliminary conclusions, analysis) that it is needless to publish. Only the recommendations, in the form of a motion or a resolution, should be presented by the committee for adoption.

Our board adopts minutes of its committees as reports. Is this a good idea?

The minutes of a committee constitute the internal record of what the committee did; they should not be acted upon by the board. The committee should extract from its minutes its recommendations and present them to the board as motions in its report.

Some committees report to the board without having met, at least not properly, or with a quorum.

A committee may not act without a meeting or without a quorum (usually a majority of the members). Perhaps a committee journal (appendix C), where the committee minutes would be maintained and accessible, would help this problem.

Is it proper that our president debates items of business at board meetings and also votes? We have eighteen on the board.

The president should not debate but should maintain an arms-length distance from discussion, providing facts to the meeting as appropriate. The main duty of the president during a meeting is to facilitate the meeting. The president should vote only if the vote will make a difference; if the vote is of no great consequence, the president should be reluctant to vote even then. It is good practice for presidents to maintain a neutral positions during meetings at which they preside.

May our association meet by e-mail?

Electronic mail is an excellent medium in which to gather facts and share information and opinions. However, an exchange of e-mail is not a legal meeting. All members in a meeting must be able to hear every other person participating simultaneously, and to respond immediately. Electronic mail does not meet that requirement. A combination of electronic mail and a telephone conference call is an efficient and effective way of conducting business. The telephone meeting is the legal meeting; e-mail supports it, by gathering facts and focusing opinion. Meeting by telephone should be listed as allowed in the organization's documents of authority.

Our annual meeting has not had a quorum present in at least ten years, likely not since our early years, yet we conduct business. The organization is thirty years old, and since our founding meeting our bylaws have said that a quorum is a majority of the members. We have 1,100 members; there are usually 150 in attendance. We are incorporated. What can be done?

This is a typical problem. A lawyer may be able to find a legal remedy through the courts, but an association may find it expensive. As annual meetings conducting business without quorums have gone on for years and no one has complained, at least to date, it may be considered a "common practice" of the association. The following process should be followed:

- Let all the members know in writing of the situation—highlight the problem.

- Draw attention to the fact that the problem has existed for at least ten years and must be corrected to avoid problems in the future.

- Let the members know that the bylaws will be changed at the next meeting to reduce the quorum to, say, seventy-five members.

- Encourage all members to attend.

- Hold the meeting and amend the bylaws.

It is important that all members be aware of this problem. It is important to bring it to the forefront so that any member can inquire about and object to any action the association takes. If there is a formal objection, legal counsel should be consulted. Otherwise, the members are likely in agreement with the approach outlined above to correcting this long-standing problem.

Is it a good idea to have a president-elect in the officer structure?

This is really dependant on the nature and character of an association. Having a president-elect, chosen perhaps a year or two early, provides for continuity in leadership and allows the president-elect to obtain insight into the workings of the presidency, provided the president-elect and the president agree to a close relationship. It normally works in stable associations with well established mandates and memberships that are not rapidly growing. For newer organizations that are still attempting to establish officer responsibilities and individual credentials, it is best not to provide for a president-elect in the officer structure. In this case, flexibility is required in selecting the president.

We have board members who always dominate discussions. How do we bring out the opinions of newer or shyer members?

There is no one solution to this problem. Newer members are often hesitant to put forward their opinions, because they do not know how they will be received. Others are simply reticent about speaking up. Some ideas to try are:

- Hold board training and include social interactions in which the board members can get to know each other. It is generally true that people who know each other from social or educational settings are more likely than otherwise to share opinions. Participation at the board meeting should then improve.

- Ask the reticent member to lead the meeting in prayer or the pledge to the flag, or to read the mission statement, or undertake some other such small activity.

- The presiding officer should lean to recognizing reticent members to speak before other members. The presiding officer may even approach them before meetings to ask them to comment on a subject with which they are familiar. This may instil confidence in the member and encourage them to participate more in meetings.

- Rotate discussion. This is an excellent way of getting all ideas on the table. It brings the reticent member into the fold—if the person wishes to participate.

- As a drastic measure (at the board level), limit members to speaking once per motion.

Should our association use a parliamentarian?

In certain meetings, a parliamentarian is essential. For conventions or annual meetings, it is advisable to hire a parliamentarian. Presiding officers should be permitted to choose the professional parliamentarian, because it is important that the presiding officer and parliamentarian work well together. The parliamentarian should participate in activities prior to the meeting; in that way, it may be possible to anticipate and solve most procedural problems ahead of time. Problems always arise at meetings, but they can be minimized through good planning.

The parliamentarian only advises; the presiding officer rules. It is important that the parliamentarian sit beside the presiding officer, in order to be able to advise unobtrusively. Proximity is also important if the presiding officer wishes to consult briefly with the parliamentarian. The parliamentarian should generally be passive, allowing minor infractions to continue if they do not affect the rights of members. Bringing to the attention of the presiding officer every infraction would be disruptive and probably not appreciated.

Sometimes we have media at our meetings. Sometimes they are welcome, sometimes not. How do we handle this?
Media are generally nonmembers and as such may be excluded from the meeting, through a vote of the membership. However, it is not always a good idea to exclude the media.

Reporters often have their own sources, and members may be willing to talk to them outside of the meeting setting, in which case they hear only one side of an issue. It is therefore often not a good business decision to exclude media. The best approach is to ask at the beginning of the meeting for media representatives to identify themselves. Have them go to a microphone and introduce themselves. This performs the useful function of welcoming them and more importantly lets the members know that there are reporters present and that they should govern themselves accordingly.

Depending on the nature of the association, it is important to have a healthy respect for and an open relationship with the media. If the need arises, they can be excluded by a vote.

Our secretary puts everything in the minutes—who seconds the motion, discussion, and full committee reports.
It is unnecessary to put seconds, full committee reports, or discussion in the minutes. The minutes should report what was done, not who did it, and not what was said. This parliamentary authority does not require

the name of the maker of a motion to be in the minutes; once a motion is adopted, the decision belongs to the assembly, not to any individual. See chapter 1 for what should and what should not be in the minutes.

When a motion is being withdrawn, our presiding officer always asks if the seconder is willing to withdraw the motion. Is this correct?

No, it is not correct. Once the presiding officer has stated the motion, the assembly owns it. The maker of the motion, having realized that it will be handily defeated, may make a separate motion to withdraw it. The presiding officer treats this as a request and asks if there is any objection to withdrawing the motion; if there is no objection, the original motion is withdrawn. If there is an objection, anyone may second the motion to withdraw, and the presiding officer takes a vote. There is no need to involve the seconder of the original motion.

When we spend time on an amendment and it passes, we still have to take another vote. Many of our member do not understand why we need to take the second vote.

The general rule is that if two motions have been made—say, a main motion and an amendment—two votes are required. Another general rule is that the order in which the votes are taken is opposite to that in which the motions were made. If a main motion is made and then an amendment, a vote is taken first on the amendment, then on the main motion (as amended, if the amendment passed).

An example will highlight why it is important to take the second vote. Consider a member moving to "meet on Sunday morning at 8 A.M." Now, if you as a member would rather not meet on Sunday but feel that if the group must meet that day it should do so at a reasonable time, you may move to amend by "striking 8 A.M." and "inserting 1 P.M." If this amendment passes (and you would vote for it), the time for the meeting on Sunday would be 1 P.M.—if the meeting is to be held. When the main motion—to meet on Sunday at 1 P.M.—is voted on, you would vote against it, because you do not want to meet on Sunday at all. The amendment adopted at least mitigates the inconvenience, if there is to be a meeting. Taking that second vote is crucial for you, as well as the correct procedure.

Our association requires a double-majority vote to adopt certain items of business. How do we handle amendments to motions?
The process for handling amendments on double-majority votes (chapter 10) should be stipulated in the documents of authority. It is recommended that the organization use a single-majority vote, taken in the regular assembly, to adopt amendments. The rationale is that if one constituency does not like the amendment, it should not have two opportunities to defeat it.

Depending on the nature of the organization, however, it may be possible to argue for a double-majority vote for amendments. In any case, it is imperative that the organization take a position on the subject and include its decision in a document of authority.

How do we address the president when he or she is presiding?
Address officers by their titles—"Madam President," "Mr. Secretary," "Mr. Moderator," or "Madam Chair."

This book generally uses the term "presiding officer" as more generic and modern. "Chair," or "chairman," is also appropriate, but as a rule the organizational title of the person being addressed should be used. It is a courtesy and a mark of respect toward the person who has attained the title.

Why does parliamentary procedure appear so difficult? Where can I learn more about it?
Parliamentary procedure is no more difficult than that of other professions. Rules of order are logical and follow common sense. Procedure in smaller assemblies—say, less than fifteen members—should generally be informal procedure, resorting to more formality when specifically required. The use of outdated terminology and a general fear of speaking publicly also hold people back from participating and from using procedure properly. Materials for education and training are available from (information current as of September 2002):

American Institute of
Parliamentarians
P.O. Box 2173
Wilmington, Del. 19899-2173

National Association of
Parliamentarians
213 South Main Street
Independence, Mo. 64050-3850

Phone: (302) 762-1811
Phone: (888) 664-0428
(toll-free)
Fax: (302) 762-2170
Web: http://www.
parliamentaryprocedure.org
E-mail: aip@
parliamentaryprocedure.org

Phone: (816) 833-3892
Phone: (888) NAP-2929
(toll-free)
Fax: (816) 833-3893 or
(816) 833-3413
Web: www.paliamentarians.org
E-mail: hq@nap2.org

One of our members once spoke in a denigrating manner about another member. What could have been done?

This is a serious breach of decorum (see "Discipline in Meetings," in chapter 1). The presiding officer should have immediately stepped in and stopped the speaker. Failing that, any member could have interrupted the speaker (one of the few times an interruption of a speaker is allowed) and raised a point of order. This forces the presiding officer to act—to rule on the point of order—and it brings to the attention of the meeting the serious breach of the rules. The offending speaker may then be ordered to be seated or to apologize. In the severest of possible actions, the offender may be expelled from the meeting.

Most meeting participants—and, unfortunately, most presiding officers as well—are reluctant to stop offensive speech. In many cases they do not know how to do it. It is best to act when the offense is still minor and a mild admonition from the presiding officer may be all that is required to prevent escalation of words. The process is very simple—immediate action by the presiding officer, or a point of order raised by any member.

Our association wishes to impeach our president. How do we go about it?

When contemplating removal of an officer, it is important to follow closely the organization's documents of authority. There are two ways of removing an officer from elected positions:

• Rescinding the election

• Formally charging the officer and holding a trial

Rescinding the election is an option if the officer was elected "for *x* years *or* until their successor is elected." Only the assembly that elected the officer may rescind the election, unless the documents of authority say differently. A special meeting may be held for which the announcement states as an item of business, for example, "That the election of Mr. President be rescinded." The second item on the agenda would be "The election of a president." Of course, the second item would be moot if the rescission fails. A majority vote to rescind the election of the president is required. This is the normal vote required for rescinding a previous action of the assembly.

If the bylaws are silent or state that an officer is elected "for *x* years *and* until their successor is elected," the officer must be formally charged and tried. If the association has a normal disciplinary or trial procedure, it should be followed.

When a bylaw allows a nonmember a "voice" at meetings, what exactly does that mean? Does it allow the nonmember to debate and make motions?

A "voice " given to a nonmember permits the nonmember only to discuss and debate. If the association wishes a nonmember to make motions (not recommended), it should spell this out clearly in a document of authority. A nonmember who has the right to speak must abide by the rules of debate followed by members of the body.

When two or more bylaw amendments address changes to a particular section of the bylaws, how does the presiding officer deal with conflicts between them?

The general rule is that the least inclusive amendment is dealt with first. For example, if one amendment intends to change a few words and another intends to strike out the entire section, the amendment changing the few words is dealt with first. After the first amendment is disposed of, the presiding officer takes up the second, even if the first amendment was adopted.

However, often it is not as simple as this. If an amendment that is adopted makes a subsequent amendment syntactically nonsensical, the member proposing the subsequent amendment is permitted to change its wording. This change is permitted only within the "scope of notice" of the amendment.

What is the "scope of notice" of an amendment to the bylaws?

Additional amendments proposed to an amendment during the meeting may not extend the scope of the intended change. For example, if an article in the bylaws contains a list of seven items and an amendment intends to add an eighth, it is improper to amend that bylaw amendment by adding yet another (ninth) item to the list. The presiding officer should rule the amendment out of order, or any member may raise a point of order.

APPENDIX A

~

Sample Minutes

CPPMD National Association
Quarterly Board Meeting
Hilton Hotel, Seattle

Date of Meeting: October 16, 2003
Time Convened: 8:34 A.M.
Presiding Officer: President, Marie Fisher
Secretary: Secretary, Ari Timbo
Members Present: See attached for members present and absent.

1. The president declared a quorum present.
2. Ari Timbo performed the invocation.
3. Peter Craig led the members in the pledge to the flag.
4. The minutes of the regular board meeting held July 17 in Toronto, Ont., were adopted as circulated.
5. Consent agenda. There were thirteen items on the consent agenda (see attached). The consent agenda was adopted as distributed.
6. Officers' Report
President Fisher gave a short report on her visit to Mexico and Guatemala. She also indicated that the local Seattle president,

Ms. Sarah Meechan, would be joining the meeting for lunch and would provide an update on local affairs.

Vice-President Huang provided summary information on progress with the tax situation and the federal government.

Treasurer Patrick provided the statement of income and expenses for the quarter ended August 31, 2003. He also provided a cash-flow summary to July 2004 for the members' information.

Secretary Timbo circulated his report in writing.

7. Standing Committees

Two standing committees reported, the Awards Committee and the Political Activities Committee.

Awards Committee

The chair of the Awards Committee moved on behalf of the committee, "That a yearly award for the best writings by a member in the association journal be initiated for the year 2004."

After discussion and amendment, the following motion was adopted: "That an award for the best writings by a member in the association journal be awarded every two years starting with the years January 2004 to December 2005."

The chair, on behalf of the committee, moved the following motion, "That the chapter with the greatest growth be recognized each year at the annual convention." After discussion the motion was referred back to the committee with instructions to report at the next meeting and to develop a method of gathering information on how best to gather information on chapter growth.

Note: Lunch break was taken at 11:50 A.M.

Note: Meeting reconvened at 1:40 P.M.

Political Activities Committee

The chair of the committee reported on the two bills that are being considered by the federal government and that may affect the association negatively.

The chair on behalf of the committee moved the following motion, "That we hire a lobbyist to work on our behalf for a one year period or until the legislation is disposed of, at a cost not to exceed $30,000."

A point of order was made that the board did not have the authority to hire a lobbyist and that the motion should be ruled out of order. The president ruled that the point of order was not well taken. The ruling of the president was appealed. On the appeal a counted vote was taken on the motion "Shall the decision of the president be sustained?" The vote was ten for sustaining the decision of the president, eight against. The decision was sustained, and the motion was declared in order.

The following motion was voted on: "That we hire a lobbyist to work on our behalf for a one year period or until the legislation is disposed of, at a cost not to exceed $25,000." A count was ordered on the vote. The vote was nine for, nine against the motion. The motion was defeated.

7. Special Committees. No special committees reported.

8. New Business

The following motion was moved and seconded: "That a special committee of five members of the board and two members of staff be appointed to look into and recommend to the board how best to comply with the new privacy code introduced last year and how the association might best meet the intent of the legislation." Adopted.

The president appointed: Harry Dempsey, chair, Guus VanKesteren, Iris Kay, Jill Peters and Lu Morelli. Staff members appointed were Fred Lane, executive director, and Frank Putin. Mr. Putin to act as secretary for the committee.

May Friend gave notice that she will present a motion on the board rules at the January 2003 meeting, specifically with regard to deportment and dress when board members attend official functions on behalf of the association.

The meeting adjourned at 5:05 P.M.

[Signed]

Ari Timbo

APPENDIX B

~

Report Format

Committee: Special Committee on Bonding
Cam Cameron, chair
Val Gregg
Sid Laforge
Mandate or Motion (Scope of Work)
To investigate and report to the board the type and cost of bonding instruments that may be acquired for the executive director and treasurer of the association.
Instructions

- Report at July Board meeting

- Acquire at least three quotes

- Use the treasurer and executive director as resources

Meetings
[List here the dates the committee met.]
[Also list non-members of the committee who attended.]

Analysis
[Provide information gathered, sources of information, resources used, options considered, analysis conducted and conclusions reached.]

Recommendations
[Provide recommendations and rationale for recommendations.]

Motions
[Provide motions that will be presented to the board.]

Impact
[Provide any budget impact.]
[Provide any potential impact or changes in the documents of authority.]

Attachments
[Provide any supplementary information to help the board decide.]

APPENDIX C

~

Committee Journal

Committee Name: Membership Committee
Type of Committee: Organizational/Standing
Committee Mandate and Objectives:

1. To maintain an accurate membership roll.
2. To maintain a list of statewide local organizations and their leaderships.
3. To recommend to board membership acquisition and retention programs.
4. To recommend to the annual meeting the "member of the year" award.

Committee Authority: Bylaw Article VI, sections 1 and 2. This article permits the board to assign specific duties to the committee.
Number of Members on Committee: A maximum of nine members are appointed in accordance with the bylaw.
How Members and Chair Are Appointed

1. The chair is appointed by the president and ratified by the board.
2. The chair of the committee and the president appoint the members jointly.

Terms of Office of Members and Chair: The term of office is two years. The chair may not be appointed for more than two consecutive terms.

Quorum Required to Conduct Business: A majority of the members of the committee constitutes a quorum.

Committee's Reporting Requirement

1. The committee must report at the annual meeting.
2. The committee must report its plans for the next two years at the beginning of each new administration and to the board when requested.

Current Activity

Name of Chair and Members:

Members appointed November 2001 were: Mrs. Adams, chair; Mr. Board, vice chair; Mr. Coates, secretary; Mr. Uda, Ms. Stuart, Mrs. Chan, Mrs. Jugal, Mr. Wilken, Ms. Poiter. The president is an ex officio member.

Meeting Dates:

First Tuesday, at 7 P.M., every other month starting in February, in headquarter boardroom.

Committee Plans:

Plans are as attached and as presented to the board in December 2001

List of Business Referred to the Committee:

January 6, 2002, received from the association secretary the following items of business:

1. That the membership committee recommend to the board the format and content of a membership brochure to be distributed annually to the local chamber of commerce and local businesses, along with estimates of the costs of production and distribution.
2. That the membership committee consider and recommend to the board the advantages and disadvantages of making the membership list accessible to local businesses.

Both items have to be reported back with recommendations no later than the June 2002 board meeting.

Minutes of Meetings: The minutes of membership committee 1961–2000 are maintained in archives at headquarters and are available upon request to members of the committee or to officers of the association. The current minutes, from 2001 and 2002, are in appendix A of this book.

APPENDIX D

~

Sample Convention Rules

[The following rules are provided as examples only. Organizations need to tailor their rules and meeting policy to meet their own needs. Some organizations need only a few rules, while others may need an extensive set of rules.]

Recognition and Debate

Only delegates at a microphone will be recognized to speak in debate. Other members of the association (nondelegates) may be recognized to speak at the discretion of the presiding officer or a majority vote of the assembly.

Once recognized by the presiding officer, the delegate must state his or her name and the local association represented by the delegate.

Unless asking for information or clarification, speakers shall indicate whether they speak for or against the motion.

Any person speaking may only speak once to a motion and for a maximum of four minutes. A member's remarks may be extended by a majority vote of the delegates.

Speakers shall avoid attacking other members in debate and shall avoid personal remarks.

When a speaker is speaking or has ceased speaking it is not permissible to clap or to show dissent from the speaker's remarks. Support for or dissension from a speaker's remarks may only be shown by individual members who are recognized to speak.

Voting

When called upon to vote, the members shall hold up their voting cards, unless the presiding officer or a vote of the assembly decides upon a different method.

A counted vote will be taken using the serpentine method of voting.

If the assembly orders a ballot vote, delegates shall use the ballot forms provided.

Motions

Resolutions for which insufficient notice has been given shall be considered only if a two-thirds vote of the assembly decides that the substance or timing indicates urgency.

Motions to postpone an item of business to the next meeting are permitted.

An appeal from the decision of the chair is not debatable, but the presiding officer may indicate the reason for the ruling that led to the appeal, and the person making the appeal may indicate the reason for the appeal.

Nominations and Elections

Candidates for office will be permitted to speak for a total of four minutes on their candidacies. Candidates may ask any person to speak on their behalf.

When more than two candidates run for office and the number of candidates required to be elected do not receive a majority of the votes cast, the candidate with the least number of votes shall be dropped from the next ballot, provided that at least two candidates remain on the ballot. If two or more candidates receive the same least number of votes (that is, tie for last place), all candidates will remain on the ballot.

Other

Delegates, members, and guests shall wear name badges provided by the credentials committee at all times in the convention meeting rooms and in the hallways adjacent to the rooms.

Food or drinks, other than water, are not permitted in the meeting rooms.

Vendors may not solicit business in the meeting room while the delegate assembly is in session.

Index

~

About the Author

James Lochrie is a certified professional parliamentarian. He is registered with the American Institute of Parliamentarians and is a member of the National Association of Parliamentarians. He teaches widely in the United States and Canada on all aspects of parliamentary law to professional colleagues, nonprofit organizations, and boards of directors. He is a meeting consultant for many international, state, and provincial clients, attending their annual and convention meetings as their parliamentarian and meeting advisor. He has been a volunteer member and officer of many nonprofit organizations, where he learned the importance of democratic procedure and due process for ensuring effective and efficient meetings.

He is a past president of the American Institute of Parliamentarians and has served in many positions with that prestigious organization. He has also served as a staff member at the Floyd M. Riddick Practicum at the College of William and Mary, in Williamsburg, Virginia, and as a staff member at the Richard E. Lucas Practicum at California State Polytechnic at Pomona. He was presented with the American Institute of Parliamentarians "President's Award for Writings in Parliamentary Law" for the years 1999–2000, for an article on election paradoxes.